Praise for *The God of Wild Places*

"Tony has managed to weave together into one beautiful but foreboding tapestry, the surprisingly unpredictable nature of life in the suburbs, with the unexpected but predictable cycles of nature in the wild places. I found myself leaning in toward the page and then beyond, into the counterintuitive teaching that has always been at the heart of the wisdom of the ages. I loved it!"—**Suzanne Stabile**, author of *The Path Between Us, The Journey Toward Wholeness*; host of The Enneagram Journey Podcast; and co-author of *The Road Back to You*, with Ian Morgan Cron

"Tony Jones speaks into the harsh reality of an increasingly churchless world and how the Creator can be found in unexpected ways in the glorious, wild creation. By giving us a glimpse of his own journey toward a more holistic and deeper faith, Jones is sharing his own experience of seeing God as bigger than our encultured expectations. As one who has also found peace and connection with the Divine among the wild places, I resonate with Tony's contemplations in this beautifully written memoir. I love this book as I am sure many others will."—**Peter Enns**, author of *Curveball: When Your Faith Takes Turns You Never Saw Coming*

"Tony Jones's memoir is a vivid narrative that sits the reader in his canoe, sharing his journey of reflection and wonder. Jones's search reminds me of Max from the classic story, *Where the Wild Things Are*, another journey of self-discovery in a boat, in which the reader learns when to roar and when to be silent. We need such adventures to renew our perspectives, calm our fears, and remind us that life-learning requires role models like Tony and Max. If we read carefully, they show us the way home!"—**Rabbi Dr. Joseph A. Edelheit**, author of *What Am I Missing? Questions About Being Human*

"Discomfort and risk have been nearly eliminated from our modern lives. In *The God of Wild Places*, Tony Jones challenges us to understand the deep spiritual benefits of having a greater connection to nature and the physical and emotional risks inherent in a life in the wilderness. And he reintroduces us to the spiritual act of eating wild things— something our society lost long ago."—**Mark Norquist**, founder of Modern Carnivore

"Tony certainly does not hide behind his vestments in this book. He sheds his armor, and his heartfelt honesty comes forth. His truthfulness is at times uncomfortable as truth often is. I felt this book deeply. Tony stepped from a man-made pulpit and church building with a flock following his words into a true wilderness to feel his faith unobstructed in the wild. No walls or ceilings. Pure connection. Although Tony's belief is still deep, his new point of view is making clearer his faith—his belief in family, in nature, and in himself. Never have I read a book that goes so deeply and personally into the act of hunting and meat as a healing and profound revelation. As a backpacker and canoeist, I very much connected with Tony's new point of view of celebrating reverence in the wilds."—**Sean "Shug" Emery**, backpacker, hammocker, canoeist, YouTube content maker

"In *The God of Wild Places*, Tony Jones introspectively details his own spiritual journey that took him from his own ordination as a pastor to leaving religion behind. Like millions of Americans, Jones went on a quest to find a resting place for his soul only to discover it in the wilderness of God's creation. Those who feel spiritually anxious and religiously adrift will find solace and encouragement in Tony's words." —**Ryan P. Burge**, associate professor of political science, Eastern Illinois University; and author of *The Nones: Where They Came From, Who They Are, and Where They Are Going*

"This is the story I have been waiting for Tony Jones to tell the world, in the way that only he can: an unvarnished and intimate look at his own life, his failings, his longings, and his pursuit of God. Funny, smart, and courageous, he debates his toughest character yet—himself—and finds the God who has followed him to all his wild places. Tony may have left organized religion, but he's still preaching, and church folks should listen to him."—**Lillian Daniel**, author of *Tired of Apologizing for a Church I Don't Belong To*; conference minister, United Church of Christ

"The way Tony Jones writes about God makes me want to walk out into the woods looking for my own religious experience. In this memoir, Tony does the thing that is sometimes the hardest for writers to execute, but is crucial for the reader to relate: he drops his ego and lets you really see him. His story is painful and beautiful and had this city girl wishing for a weekend in the wilderness."—**Laura Tremaine**, podcaster and author of *Share Your Stuff. I'll Go First (10 Questions To Take Your Friendships To The Next Level)*

"Tony Jones walked away from church and out into the woods, and his thoughtful reflections on that soulful transition are compelling, engaging, and full of the kind of transcendent faith that this world needs now, more than ever."—**Phil Zuckerman**, associate dean, Pitzer College, and author of *Living the Secular Life, Society without God, and Beyond Doubt*

"Tony Jones's book, centered in his experiences of hunting, is challenging. Especially for someone who has developed a deep, intimate relationship with deer. But I kept reading because I felt compelled to understand. Told with vulnerability and straightforward honesty, Jones weaves a theology of predation into his experiences of both the numinous presence in and between all things and the reciprocity of relationship that can be experienced in the act of hunting. His book helped me to weave some threads of my own journey as a gatherer into a more broad and more spiritual story of aliveness."—**Victoria Loorz**, author, *Church of the Wild: How Nature Invites Us into the Sacred*

The God
of Wild Places

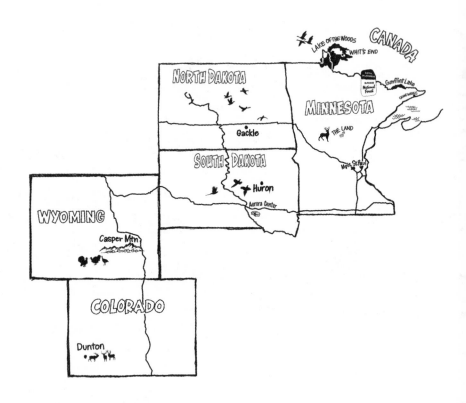

The God
of Wild Places

Rediscovering the Divine in the Untamed Outdoors

TONY JONES

ROWMAN & LITTLEFIELD
Lanham • Boulder • New York • London

Published by Rowman & Littlefield
An imprint of The Rowman & Littlefield Publishing Group, Inc.
4501 Forbes Boulevard, Suite 200, Lanham, Maryland 20706
www.rowman.com

86-90 Paul Street, London EC2A 4NE

Distributed by NATIONAL BOOK NETWORK

British Library Cataloguing in Publication Information Available

Library of Congress Cataloging-in-Publication Data

978-1-5381-8444-8 (cloth)
978-1-5381-8445-5 (electronic)

♾™ The paper used in this publication meets the minimum requirements of American National Standard for Information Sciences—Permanence of Paper for Printed Library Materials, ANSI/NISO Z39.48-1992.

DEDICATED TO

Doug
Jorge
Harry
and Larry

who led me outdoors.

Gradually the streamers of rose and mauve in the east changed to gold, and then the sun burst over a spruce-etched hill. At that moment the river was transformed into a brilliant crystalline boulevard stretching to infinity. The air was mountain air that morning, and my feet were winged. I was in the forbidden land, land of the spirits, a place to approach with awe and perhaps with prayer.

—Sigurd Olson, *The Singing Wilderness*

Contents

INTRODUCTION

Wilderness is mainly wilderness because it's hard to get to and rough to travel through, and the particularities of nature have to be known to enjoy it in any viable way. There is a secretive melancholy among those who love and know the wilderness. It is an experience like religious conversion that has to be undergone to be understood.

—Jim Harrison, "Old, Faithful, and Mysterious"

PAUL PICKED ME UP ON A SATURDAY MORNING IN MAY. I WAS A seventh grader; he was a part-time youth minister at our church who bore an uncanny resemblance to John Denver. Paul drove a busted-up old van that he'd sheathed in Rust-Oleum spray paint to forestall the inevitable. Various lengths of PVC pipe rattled around in the back of the van, accoutrements of his side hustle installing lawn sprinklers.

Paul had invited me to give the offertory prayer on Youth Sunday, the annual worship service at our church celebrating middle and high schoolers. Instead of the organ and choir, a band of teenagers led the music that morning, the sermon was geared toward a younger crowd, and some kid got picked to pray over the money collected in the offering plates. In 1981, that kid was me.

My mom sent me off to breakfast with a blank index card from her recipe box. Paul helped me compose the 10-second prayer, which I would read the following morning in front of the congregation. That task accomplished, Paul looked at me across the plastic McDonald's table and, surely just trying to make conversation with an awkward adolescent, asked me what I wanted to do when I grew up.

"I want to be a minister."

Although those words had never before exited my mouth, I knew that they were the truest words I'd ever spoken.

The next morning, dressed in khaki pants and an Izod shirt, I spoke into a microphone in a church sanctuary for the first time. Over the following years, church was my second home, a place where I felt comfortable and competent and confident—valuable commodities as a middle schooler. I'd pull all-nighters there, arranging slides in carousel trays and syncing them with music on a reel-to-reel tape player, to be shown at youth group. I knew the inventory in every storage closet in the building. During high school I taught Sunday school to junior high boys, mumbling through the unit on the "sin of masturbation." By college, I was the summer intern. My trajectory was set: I was going to spend my life in church.

A decade later, as a newly married, freshly-minted minister, I started pastoring in that same congregation. And shortly thereafter, my first book came out—a "minor classic in youth ministry," according to one reviewer—followed by more books and more invitations to preach. Journalists called me for quotes. At church conferences, I rarely bought a meal, the tab instead picked up by publishers and agents who were courting me, or by fans who wanted to express their gratitude and pick my brain. It was a heady time: when I wasn't preaching and leading prayers in my own church, I was on an airplane to preach and pray in other, bigger pulpits.

I prayed at home too, but those were different: panicky pleas that God would somehow fix my broken marriage. I staved off the creeping sense that my petitions weren't really working. I thought back on the feeling when, as a child, I'd gone forward during an altar call at church camp—I asked Jesus into my heart, as directed, and I felt something real: a bodily experience of the divine that was unmistakable and un-deniable. But two decades removed from that very real experience, it served me like one good hand hold on a rock climbing wall. The problem was that my other three limbs hung without purchase, and I was losing grip on that singular moment with God. Much of my self-identity—both spiritual and vocational—was rooted in that one event, and in the church that had facilitated it. The fact that I couldn't replicate it worried me—or, it should have, if I had allowed myself to consider it, which I didn't. God wasn't talking back to me when I prayed, but I paid the silence no heed. During those early years of pastoring, around the age of 30, I went hunting for the first time. To this day, I don't quite know the origin of my desire to hunt, but a guy in the congregation named Doug hunted a lot, and he offered to take me. We made a plan to visit his cabin on Lake of the Woods for the opening of Ontario duck hunting season in mid-September.

Doug and I loaded gear into his minivan and drove north out of Minneapolis. Six hours later, we rolled into the yard of his cousin's pre-fabricated home in Baudette, Minnesota, on the border with Canada, just past the statue of the giant walleye, and he let his dogs out for a run. Then we drove over the Baudette-Rainy River International Bridge into Canada to buy hunting licenses, remote border crossing permits, and permits to transport our shotguns over the dotted line on the map that bisects the giant lake. We also bought some Cuban cigars that we stashed under our seats, and we crossed back into the States.

That night we loaded Doug's "Big Boat," a 27-foot Sportcraft Fisherman with a 340-horsepower Mercruiser engine, a vessel large enough to ply the expanse of Lake of the Woods that locals call "Big Water." The next morning, Doug backed the boat out of the boathouse and slowly navigated northwest along the Rainy River, the United States to our port side and Canada starboard. We cleared the no-wake zone and entered the lake; he throttled the engine up, planing out the boat.

Lake of the Woods used to be little more than a swamp, residue left behind by the glacial Lake Agassiz, a 150,000-square mile behemoth that retreated 10,000 years ago. In the late 1800s, a dam was erected at Kenora, Ontario, and the water level rose by three feet, transforming the swamp into a lake. Even so, it's shallow, and, with over 14,500 islands and countless rock outcroppings spread over its 1,679 square miles, treacherous to navigate.

Big Water, however, is treacherous not for its shallowness but for its depth, and for the fact that as a vast expanse of water stretching from east to west, wind whips waves into a froth. Doug tacked the boat so that we'd be headed either directly into or away from the waves. With each swell, the Big Boat's bow climbed then slapped down. Dalton and Dallas, Doug's black Labs, curled up at his feet under the pilot's chair.

Having crossed the eastern expanse of Big Water, we approached the southern tip of Bigsby Island and began to circumnavigate its shoals counterclockwise. Doug told me to climb onto the bow and hang out over the railing. I looked down into the water for rocks that could slash open the boat's hull, shouting over the roar of the engine and waving my arms if I saw one, even though Doug, not the most patient guy, ran the boat fast enough that avoiding hazards seemed unlikely. When we heard a vicious scrape on the underside of the boat, Doug barked at me to do a better job.

A polyp of land juts out of the east side of Bigsby Island, and across a 100-yard channel of water sits Gooseneck Island, upon which was perched Whit's End, Doug's family cabin. The half-log siding was painted bright red with white window frames—a cottage balanced atop a massive slab of granite, the remnants of some prehistoric volcano. Doug eased the Big Boat up to the dock, and I disembarked and tried to remember the clove hitch knot he'd taught me four hours earlier when we left Baudette. I couldn't, and I wrestled with whether it would be worse to admit my ignorance of ship knots or take a chance on the Big Boat floating away in the night due to my ignorance. I decided to tie a foursquare and take my chances. But Doug inspected my knot and chastised me and re-taught me the clove hitch, which I promptly re-forgot. We unloaded the Big Boat, opened the cabin, and Doug fired up the generator out back. He claimed the master bedroom, and I dropped my duffel in one of the smaller bedrooms. We unloaded our cooler into the propane refrigerator.

Two upturned duck boats rested on the shore. We flipped the larger of the two, unearthing bags of decoys, oars, push-poles, and outboard motors.

Ducks flew everywhere. I kept looking skyward at the flocks screaming over the channel like squadrons of fighter jets.

People, however, were scarce—maybe once during our four-day stay we saw a boat in the distance. When we were out on the hunt, we heard neither a motor nor the report of a shotgun. I was as far from civilization as I'd ever been. And I loved it. The sense that I was in control—surely a false sense—fell away on the labyrinthine lake. The fundamental uncontrollability of the world overwhelmed me. But instead of feeling frightened or anxious, I felt alive, more fully alive than I did in the mundanities of my everyday life.

Most of us don't quit church (or temple, synagogue, or mosque) in a huff, storming out mid-sermon, vowing never to return. Instead, we slide away slowly, attending less and less often until one day we're forced to admit, "I don't go to church anymore." These days, us non-churchgoers are the fastest growing segment of the American religious landscape—according to the Pew Survey, nearly 45 percent of Americans aged 40 and younger claim no religious affiliation, a dramatic increase from past generations that shows no signs of abating. Maybe not coincidentally, the trend-line of Americans' participation in outdoors activities is headed in the opposite direction, growing significantly over the past 15 years.

My own personal trend-lines match. The line that measures church attendance is descending, and it intersects on the graph with an ascending line that measures my outdoors activity; as my religion has waned, my love of the wilderness has waxed; the more time I've spent in wild places, the less I've spent in church. Given the choice of taking a hike or paddling a canoe or hunting for pheasants versus sitting in a pew for a worship service, I'll choose the hike/paddle/hunt option one hundred times out of one hundred. It's like the sign my buddy has at his lake cabin: "I'd rather be sitting in a fishing boat thinking about God than sitting in church thinking about fishing."

And I'm not alone. Many of us experience God in nature. Cliché? Maybe. But that doesn't make it untrue. God really is there, in the wild, untamed places, among the flora and fauna that cohabit this planet with us.

What follows is what I've learned since I walked out of the church and into the woods. Some of the lessons overlap with what I was taught in my many years in organized religion. But somehow they're more poignant, more beautiful when they're learned in nature.

Think of religion as a trellis.

Human beings have experiences of transcendence, as reported by shamans, sages, philosophers, preachers, and everyday persons from time immemorial. We touch the ineffable, the divine, the numinous, and then we search for language to describe what is essentially indescribable.

Some among us—the poets and painters and songwriters and novelists—find original ways to describe their contact with the transcendent. But most of us do not. Instead, we look for existing linguistic structures that approximate our encounter with the divine, that give us handholds and footholds as we attempt to climb what the sixth century monk St. John Climacus called the Ladder of Divine Ascent.

Few of us are strong enough to reach the heavens without assistance. Religion provides a structure up which the vines of our spiritual experiences can grow. The liturgies and hymns and prayers and verses were composed by others, but they approximate my experiences well enough to be a comfort, a framework, a scaffolding—a trellis—for my faith to climb.

Until they're not.

I built a trellis in my garden—real, not metaphorical. I pounded fenceposts on either side of the raised garden bed and zip-tied a section of cyclone fence between them. Beans and squash climbed the trellis, as planned. After a couple summers, the fenceposts bent inward under the weight of the crops, so I stabilized them by affixing braces to hold them upright. That lasted a couple more years. Eventually I had to build a new trellis.

I don't know if my religion trellis rotted over time or if my quest for the divine outgrew it, but at some point the orderliness of religion no longer served me. In fact, instead of supporting my growth, it held me back, hemmed me in.

So I abandoned the trellis. Not all at once, but over time. I left the orderly pews and numbered hymns for the chaotic woods and muddy sloughs.

Annie Dillard, obviously in a fit, wrote,

> On the whole, I do not find Christians, outside of the catacombs, sufficiently sensible of conditions. Does anyone have the foggiest idea what sort of power we so blithely invoke? Or, as I suspect, does no one believe a word of it? The churches are children playing on the floor with their chemistry sets, mixing up a batch of TNT to kill a Sunday morning. It is madness to wear ladies' straw hats and velvet hats to church; we should all be wearing crash helmets. Ushers should issue life preservers and signal flares; they should lash us to our pews. For the sleeping god may wake someday and take offense, or the waking god may draw us out to where we can never return.[1]

You know where people wear helmets and life preservers? Where they carry signal flares? Outdoors, in the wilderness.

And like Ms. Dillard says, if you venture out to meet the God of wild places, you may never return.

Vestments

Wilderness. The word itself is music.

—Edward Abbey, *Desert Solitaire*

I CLIMB IN JORGE VICUNA'S TRUCK WRAPPED IN SO MANY LAYERS against the cold South Dakota wind that I can barely bend my joints. The stiff leather of my boots fights my frigid fingers as I loop the laces around eyelet hooks. I check the back of the cab for my equipment: two shotguns, ammo, water for the dogs, more layers of clothing.

I'm geared up like a soldier headed into combat: chaps, vest, and boots; hat, protective glasses, and earplugs custom-molded to my aural features. My pockets bulge with shotgun shells, and the remote control for an electric dog collar is clipped to my chest. I've brought along three pairs of gloves, prepared for changing conditions.

I'm wearing all this gear to hunt a bird, the Mongolian ring-neck-type common pheasant cock (*Phasianus colchius*). First introduced to North America in the eighteenth century for the purpose of game hunting, the pheasant didn't get established on our continent until the late nineteenth century when several batches were imported by Owen Denny, the U.S. consul general in Shanghai, who released them in Oregon. But it turns out this bird thrives in the Upper Plains biome, so they migrated east. Now over a million pheasant roosters are shot by hunters in South Dakota each year.

We load our dogs into the back of the cab, and the Dodge 2500 diesel engine roars to life. Jorge backs it down his icy driveway and pulls onto Ohio Avenue. We take a left on 9th Street and pass Nebraska,

Colorado, Montana, Nevada, Arizona, Michigan, and Minnesota Avenues. Three of the four corners at 9th and Lincoln, our next stop sign, boast churches. As we pass the town's baseball fields, leaving the city of Huron behind us, the road changes from pavement to gravel, but Jorge doesn't slow down.

Into the checkerboard of Middle America we rocket. Every quarter section we pass a north-south road, and every fourth road is marked with a stop sign, in spite of the fact that we can see at least half-a-mile in each direction. Jorge bemoans the stops as a conspiracy of petroleum and brake pad companies: "Do you know how much it takes for a semi loaded with corn or soybeans to come to a complete stop and then get going again? Every mile?!?" He says this in spite of being t-boned and almost killed at one of these intersections 20 years ago, the memory of that accident instigating another diatribe about corruption in the insurance industry. He sips from a bottle of Gatorade, cursing the damage that radiation and chemotherapy have wrought on his salivary glands.

Jorge manages thousands of acres of South Dakota farmland, most for the offspring of deceased farmers, sons and daughters who've de-camped to big cities but still reap the profits of this rich soil. As far as I can tell, he's the lone Chilean in Beadle County, having met his Midwestern wife, Connie, when she worked for the Peace Corps in the 1980s; his South American accent sticks out like a giant pigweed in a field of corn.

We stop a quarter-mile short of his own quarter-section of land to plan our attack. Jorge wants me to get out with my yellow Lab, Albert, and hike north and then west. He will drive a bit farther and then walk due north along a barbed wire fence. I exit the truck, careful to close the door quietly by pushing it until the latch clicks and then leaning on it until it's flush with the jamb—I've been scolded many times for slamming doors and alerting pheasants to our presence.

Albert and I move through the snow. In the roadside ditch it's chest-high, and I lose sight of Albert under a drift. Using the stock of my shotgun as a crutch, I surmount the other side of the ditch, where the snow is only knee-high. I'm breathing heavily and I can feel sweat running down my chest and back in spite of a wicked wind that bites at my face. The blinding sun bounces off a trillion snowflakes frosting this soybean field.

Tufts of grass along the fence line will shelter pheasants—at least that's our working theory. Although Jorge is 200 yards away from me, I can see the speck of a pheasant flying away from him, and a second later the pop-pop of two shotgun blasts reaches me, the speed of sound trailing the speed of light. I'm guessing he missed, though he may have dropped one that I didn't see. I keep trudging toward him, cracking through the snow crust with each step, occasionally falling to my knees.

Albert gallops before me, his nose to the snow. When he exceeds the 40-yard range of my shotgunning proficiency, I whistle him back, and when he's not hot on the scent of a bird, he complies.

Seeing Jorge's progress along the fence, I alter my angle and quicken my step, hoping to intersect with him at a slough of unmowed grass that bulges into the barren field like a pregnant belly. On winter days like this, pheasants wander these farm fields, scratching for remnant crops beneath the snow; and on winter nights they roost in grass or cattails, burrowing under the snow for thermal warmth and shelter from predators—the life of a pheasant is a constant battle for survival.

As I approach Jorge's position, I slow my pace. My glasses fog up, unable to reconcile my body's steamy heat with South Dakota's winter cold. Jorge waves to me and points toward Benton, indicating that his Springer spaniel is showing signs of birdiness. I quietly call Albert to heel with a finger on the button that will send a prick of electricity into his neck should he choose to ignore me.

A cackle, the telltale sound of a pheasant rooster, precedes the explosion of a bird from the snow, its iridescent green head, red face, and white choker confirming that it's the male of the species and therefore legal to shoot. Jorge and I fire simultaneously. The majestic creature tumbles back to earth, not unlike how Alexander Pope sang of a similar moment in 1713,

> See! from the brake the whirring pheasant springs,
> And mounts exulting on triumphant wings:
> Short is his joy; he feels the fiery wound,
> Flutters in blood, and panting beats the ground.[1]

Albert breaks from heel and races toward the quarry as though shot from a cannon. He grabs the bird in his jaws and bullets back to me, dropping the rooster at my feet and nosing it around until I grab it and deposit it into the game pouch built into my vest.

I've hunted pheasants with groups large and small, but this is my favorite way to chase the bird: just Jorge and me and our two dogs on a winter day, late in the season. The crowds of orange-clad hunters have gone home, chased away by snow and cold. "Only the smart birds are left," Jorge calls out to me, implying that the less intelligent roosters have already been shot. "I missed that wily one," he confesses.

Among a cohort of unlikely friends in my life, Jorge is the un-likeliest. We met in 2012. My ministry career had collapsed, victim to forces both in and out of my control, and my faith was not far behind. Although drawn to hunting, I lacked the connections essential to finding fruitful plots of land. So I posted a barter offer on the internet: I'd preach for free in exchange for hunting opportunities. Mother Jean, rector of Grace Episcopal Church in Huron, South Dakota, emailed me and offered to connect me with a hunter in her congregation if I'd preach to her little flock. When I first cruised past the World's Largest Pheasant on the outskirts of Huron, I took it as a favorable omen. Jorge graciously hosted me that weekend, as he has many times since. And I preached at Mother Jean's church, as I have every year since.

Jorge and I hunt together still, taking nothing for granted. His asymmetrical face bears the evidence of surgeons who've carved away at cancerous malignancy, and my soul carries spiritual scar tissue into which lifeblood will never again flow.

For Jorge and me, hunting is a sacred recital of our own mortality. He and I come from very different places, but we have one important thing in common: we'd rather be outdoors than indoors. It took me some time to get there, to accept the truth that my spirituality is rooted in the wilderness. In fact, it took trauma to push me out of the ordered sanctuary of organized religion and into the chaos of wild places.

Somewhere in a storage bin in my basement sits a framed photo that I recently took off the wall. In it, I'm leaning forward with an ecstatic smile, standing in the doorway to the sanctuary of the church that was long my spiritual home, surrounded by my three favorite high school teachers—they'd come to witness my ordination. That snapshot was taken on September 7, 1997, and at the time it was the culmination of everything I'd ever wanted. In the ceremony that followed, I'd had hands laid on me by a variety of clergy, and a friend from seminary who'd flown in from California preached a commissioning sermon. Then came a litany of prayers, and my investiture as a Reverend. The deacons of the church draped over me a robe that they'd purchased as an ordination gift: a black Geneva gown. Then my parents hung over my shoulders their gift: an academic hood, fringed in scarlet for my master of divinity degree. Finally, a sweet 90-year-old parishioner named Kris handed me a starched white preaching collar with two tabs, to be worn around my neck and out over my robe in the style of the Puritans. She told me that tabs represented the Old and New Testaments, which I would be proclaiming the rest of my life. I was fully vested.

I grew up at this church, envying the clergy in their august robes, preaching and praying and presenting the weekly announcements and handing out communion. Faith was the defining characteristic of my self-identity. And since being a minister is the apotheosis of faith, professional ministry seemed the obvious choice if I wanted to maintain that identity into adulthood. Even in my youth, I knew adults who'd been zealous about their faith early in life, only to watch it cool as they aged—hot lava hardening into stone—adults who'd settled into patterns of weekly attendance and giving but who showed no outward evidence that their faith made the least bit of difference in their daily lives; they showed no "fruit of the spirit," to quote the Apostle Paul. Like Paul, and unlike the adults I saw in the pews on Sunday, I resolved to maintain my zeal, and these vestments would serve to ziplock my devotion.

In the years leading to that moment, I'd done everything an aspiring minister was supposed to: I taught Sunday school, served as a summer camp counselor, and volunteered at vacation Bible school. I took guitar lessons, honing a required skill for leading praise and worship. I read everything from Thomas Aquinas to Pat Robertson. In college, I joined one campus Bible study, and then another. I attended evangelism conferences and witnessed on the streets. The summer after my freshman year, I returned to Minnesota and got my commercial driver's license so that I could drive a school bus full of church kids to the amusement park and the miniature golf course. I lectured my parents, warning them to repent of their pro-choice opinions. Back at college, I was tapped to emcee the weekly meetings of the largest Christian ministry on campus.

Then, immediately after college, I enrolled at Fuller Seminary. I packed everything I owned into my brand new Ford Probe and drove from Minnesota to Pasadena, California. For three years I learned Greek and Hebrew, took preaching classes, and worked at a church.

After graduation, I served as a missionary on the Pine Ridge Indian Reservation for three years, and it was there and then that Christianity made the most sense to me. Week after week, busloads of high school kids trucked out to the southwestern corner of South Dakota, where I'd receive them, bunk them in Wounded Knee District School, and send them out each morning to work with God's blessing. I drove an old, manual-transmission F-150 that everyone on the Rez knew as Big Red; most days I'd park it in the dirt lot at Pinky's Store and sit outside on the shaded side of the building, drinking coffee out of Styrofoam cups with the old Lakota men, our chairs tipped back against the wall.

The missions tasks I accomplished did not change the hard realities of the reservation—we painted houses and ran kids' club and built a basketball court—but I was serving, acting out my faith in ways that were appreciated and that gave me meaning.

"Go down to the Catholic Church," Pinky told me one day. "There's a wake."

"But I don't know the family," I protested.

"Doesn't matter. It's what you do. You're a pastor in this town now."

She handed me a pack of Marlboros, explaining the sacredness of tobacco and telling me to give it to the family as a gift.

I did it. I did everything that Pinky told me to do. I'd been to seminary and learned how to be a minister, but during my years on the reservation, I learned how to be a Christian. The work was never-ending, but I didn't get tired. Summer days were desert-hot, but I happily pulled on jeans and boots, climbed in my un-air-conditioned truck, only able to grip the searing steering wheel with gloves on, and set out for work that fulfilled me. I preached to the groups of white kids. But to the Lakota, I listened. At the conclusion of my time on Pine Ridge, Pinky and the residents of Manderson, South Dakota, made me an honorary member of the tribe, gave me an Indian name, and presented me with the tribal flag—my first ordination.

The mission organization grew, and I hired other staffers to launch other sites, including a woman about my age who served on a reservation in Wyoming. We shared an exuberance for the faith and the work, and we fell in love over the summer of 1996.

Then, that fall, I received the call for which I'd always hoped: my church asked me to come home and be one of their ministers. I joined the church staff and started on the process of getting ordained, which culminated in written statements defending my faith and vocation and oral arguments before a council of local clergy who examined my fitness for ministry. They approved of me, and, after stopping to take the aforementioned photo, we proceeded into the sanctuary. I was ordained and vested with the apparel of my sacerdotal station.

The Geneva gown in which I was robed used to be a protest. Rejecting the pomp of Roman Catholic vestments, the first Protestant preachers wore their work-a-day clothes into the pulpit, and because they were among the educated class, that meant black gowns. Everyday fashion has changed over the centuries, but church fashion hasn't. What had once been considered ordinary is now the height of formality.

The anachronistic robe suited me. I loved the velvet panels that ran the length of the front. I appreciated that the deacons had chosen for me the model with buttons, because Puritans don't have zippers. I bleached and starched and ironed the collar each week. I enjoyed the bulk of fabric around my neck, like a plumber's coupling clamp, cranked tight, providing the strength needed to pour forth the words of God. And although my master's hood filled me with pride, I envied the longer hoods and chevroned sleeves of my colleagues who held doctorates. Someday, I thought, I'll earn those.

We'd huddle in the narthex on Sunday mornings, clergy in robes and lay deacons in business suits, and say a quick prayer outside the sanctuary. Then, to the first stanza of the opening hymn, we'd stride down the center aisle, stepping from the red carpet onto the parquet platform, and take our seats on the wooden benches to either side of the pulpit.

As much as I loved normal Sundays, nothing could compare to the holiest days. On Christmas Eve, candelabra with two hundred flames lit the room as we processed in to the strains of "Joy to the World." And on Easter a lone trumpet pealed out the first notes of "Christ the Lord Is Risen Today," and I practically floated down the aisle.

This was where I was meant to be, *who* I was meant to be.

My dad loved that I was a minister, for I followed in the footsteps of a storied clergyman in the family, his great-grandfather. In the Jerusalem Cemetery in Judson Township, a postage stamp in the corner of a sunny cornfield, sits a decorous and understated family plot, at the center of which stands a monument to the Rev. W. Machno Jones.

Born in 1845 in Penmachno, Northern Wales, in the Gwydyr Forest of Snowdonia, by age 19 he'd been trained for the ministry, and he emigrated to the United States. He found his way to southwestern Minnesota, a land full of his fellow Welshmen. On account of the abundance of William Joneses in that neck-of-the-woods, he went by the nickname Machno, his hometown.

The Jerusalem Welsh Calvinistic Methodist (*Methodistiad Calfinaidd*) Church had been formed in 1858 and met in the log cabin home of Owen Roberts on the farm of Humphrey Jones—so says a commemorative plaque, pockmarked from shotgun pellets, standing at the edge of that farm field. The Reverend William Machno Jones, it reads, Jerusalem's first full-time minister, began his pastorate in March 1871.

On Sunday, September 10, 1876, Machno was walking to church when two rough-looking men on horseback stopped him. He wore the preaching bands of a parson, so the men asked him for a sermon, which he happily delivered as they sat in their saddles. The homily concluded, the men offered the preacher money, but Machno refused. The ruffians rode off. Machno later realized that the men were Frank and Jesse James, four days and seventy miles removed from their unsuccessful robbery of the First National Bank in Northfield, during which the rest of their gang was captured or killed.

Photos of Machno show a stern man with a bushy gray goatee and sad eyes. He'd convinced his brother, John, to join him in the States. But John, who didn't know English, alighted from the train at the wrong stop, in Dodge, Wisconsin, where he was robbed and poisoned to death. Back in Wales, the men's father blamed Machno for John's murder and never communicated with his son again.

Machno retired from the ministry in 1891. He was so beloved by his congregation that they raised enough money—$101.50—for two gold watches, one of which he gave to his wife, Alice. A book titled *The Welsh in Minnesota* (1895) says of him, "He has now retired to his beautiful farm near Lake Crystal to enjoy a short vacation. Mr. Jones is an able and effective preacher and pastor and is in the noonday of his strength. He is also possessed of an excellent Christian spirit."[2]

I've visited his grave at the Jerusalem Cemetery. On the face of his tombstone is carved a verse of a Welsh hymn,

> Mi gysgaf hun yn dawel
> Dros ennyd yn y gravel
> Nes dattod trefn y rhod
>
> [I will sleep slumber quietly,
> For a while in the gravel,
> Until the order of the sky unravels]

And the top reads: HE PREACHED THE GOSPEL FOR 52 YS.

Religion has provided a framework for my family as far back as we can trace. Machno's grandson, Ralph, and his wife, Florence, moved a couple counties north of Judson, to Gaylord, Minnesota, where Ralph bought a Ford dealership from its Jewish proprietor who decided that residing in a county full of German immigrants probably wasn't a great idea in the late 1930s. Ralph and Florence joined the Congregationalist church in town. Meanwhile, my maternal grandparents, Bower and Jane, gathered a few dozen married couples and founded a Congregationalist church of their own in the burgeoning Minneapolis suburb of Edina.

In Gaylord, Ralph mowed the church lawn and Florence placed a fresh-cut bouquet of flowers on the altar each Saturday night so that every Sunday morning would smell like Easter. In Edina, Bower chaired the church council and Jane was a deacon. Their kids, my parents, met at Carleton College, and before long they, too, were married and sitting on the church council and serving as deacons, even playing the holy family in the Christmas pageant with my infant brother, Ted, cast as the Baby Jesus, while my other brother, Andrew, and I did time as impatient shepherds.

Decades later, when I walked up to the front of that same sanctuary to be ordained, and stood on the same spot at which I'd been baptized and confirmed, I completed the holiness trifecta. It was everything I'd ever wanted.

That same year, I did other things I was supposed to do. I married the woman I'd fallen in love with the previous summer. We bought a house. We got a dog. All the pieces fit together, Tetris shapes falling into their pre-ordained slots.

The vestments of traditional, mainline Protestantism fit me perfectly, and I wore them well. They signal education and privilege. Not unlike the judicial robes they mimic, they communicate not conversation but monologue, soliloquy, judgments rendered. The robe and collar provided me a bulwark against rebuttal, archaic attire that signaled an ancient and unquestioned authority. Just watch: the congregation stands when I stand, they sit when I sit, and they turn to the page in the hymnal that I tell them to.

The apparati of religion went beyond the dress. I also mastered the speech patterns—prayers prayed in an earnest whisper, sermons delivered with poignancy and pregnant pauses, announcements given with a smile and a laugh—the verbiage of the clerical class. A laminated CLERGY sign on my dashboard permitted me to park in the red zone at hospitals. The local country club comped me membership because it looks good to have pastors in the clubhouse. The government even rewarded me, granting me a clergy tax break on housing expenses.

I loved all of it.

I'd clip the lavaliere mic onto the velvet panel on the front of my gown, slide the battery pack into my pants pocket and, through a slit in the right side of my robe, flip the switch on when it was my turn to talk. The walls of the sanctuary had been acoustically designed to contain the roar of its massive organ, and I loved hearing my amplified voice reverberate around the room. I loved standing in the high pulpit, designed to look like the prow of a ship, upon which is affixed a small brass plaque that quotes John 12:21 in King James English: "Sir, we would see Jesus." I loved telling people what to believe about God. I loved when the congregation laughed at my jokes. And I loved standing in the narthex, shaking hands and receiving compliments and getting little-old-lady hugs and being told how great my sermon was.

A dozen years after my ordination, as part of a divorce and custody fight, a court-appointed psychologist would write in her report, "Mr. Jones' profile reflects both a marked narcissistic tendency and significant anxiety. While he projects self-confidence, this is likely to mask a deeper anxiety about his self-worth." Over the course of those years, the glow of ordination day had dimmed, and rather than deal with the tendencies and anxieties that would contribute to the dissolution of the marriage, I became an expert mask-wearer.

What they tell you at seminary, in defense of the clerical vestments, is that the robe and collar hide your uniquenesses and your flaws, allowing the congregation to hear the word of God instead of getting hung up on the color of your necktie or the cut of your skirt. My long, black gown hid something else: my failures in a marriage that was destroying me, flaws that I confessed to no one, opting instead to work even harder at fulfilling the ministerial role that came with an implicit promise of peace and salvation. I focused my efforts on the heavenly, the spiritual, and the immaterial. Meanwhile the actual, material world was collapsing around me.

During those same years, I mastered another version of religion as well, one in its ascendancy. Even as I fit comfortably in the elitist garb of mainline Protestantism, I simultaneously slid into the contemporary casual of American evangelicalism. My first book came out with an evangelical publishing house, and speaking invitations rolled in. In this crowd, coats and ties were frowned upon, and clerical robes considered relics of a papist past. Here, Baby Boomers wore khakis and GenXers jeans. I stepped down from the pulpit and spoke without notes, as I'd been taught at a Dynamic Communicators Workshop. And I looked the other way at the misogyny and homophobia that was baked into the cake of evangelicalism, because my career was on the rise and I told myself that I could change it from the inside. I was telling myself a similar story about my marriage.

By 2003, having served seven years as a pastor, I headed east for a Ph.D., finally after those chevrons. I quickly noticed a sartorial pecking order at Princeton Seminary: masters students wore shorts and t-shirts, doctoral candidates donned khakis and collared shirts, and professors sported coats and ties. I played along.

With two small children, it was a big move and a big financial risk, but my spouse disliked being a pastor's wife almost as much as she disliked my family, so we welcomed a change of scenery. With the move east, we hoped to hit the reset button on everything, including our struggling union.

To save money, I packed most of what we owned into a U-Haul truck in August, drove 1,200 miles, unloaded everything into our garden-level apartment in married student housing, flew back to Minnesota, and drove the same 1,200 miles with the family in our Ford Windstar minivan.

The change of venue did not fix our problems. It never does.

The following spring, my wife and children flew back to Minnesota for the summer, and I drove home over the course of two weeks, stopping at speaking gigs I'd booked en route to make some desperately needed cash. While driving in Nashville, my flip-phone rang.

"The kids and I are not going back to Princeton," she said.

"What do you mean?" I asked. "Of course you're going back. We're all going back in the fall. When we made this decision, we knew it was a four-year commitment."

"No, the kids and I are staying in Minnesota. And we're moving back into the house, so you need to kick out the renters."

"I signed them to a one-year lease. I can't kick them out after nine months. Plus, we can't afford the mortgage without any income."

"I don't care. I'm moving back into the house. I'll tell them myself."

"What am I supposed to do about school?" I asked, panic gripping my chest as I contemplated missing my kids' firsts: first day in kindergarten, first goal in a soccer game, first choir concert.

"I guess drop out. Or commute. I don't really care. I'm not going back. And the kids are staying with me."

Later that summer, I flew back to New Jersey, packed everything into the back of a U-Haul, and drove it 1,200 miles to Minnesota. I commuted by air the balance of that year. Since commuting was not technically allowed by the school, I was required to keep an apartment in married student housing. My bed was a sleeping bag on an air mattress, and my desk was a door set on two sawhorses that I'd found leaning against a dumpster.

When I finally completed my Ph.D. many years later, I didn't don my cap and gown. I didn't receive my hood or add chevrons to my robe. I didn't even bother to go back to New Jersey for commencement—instead I was paddling a canoe on a lake.

When I received that robe, I could not imagine what my life would end up looking like, divorced from the religion and the ordination that had afforded me so much meaning and self-worth for so many years. Today my clergy gown hangs in the dark recesses of a hall closet, along with the yellowed clergy collar, pushed aside by outdoors gear which now hangs at the center of my life.

The current movement of people like me dropping out of church didn't happen overnight. The trend goes back several centuries in Western civilization. The Industrial Revolution and the Scientific Revolution chipped away at the authority of the church, which had already been weakened by the Reformation, a campaign that both rehabilitated the church and ironically initiated its long demise.[3] This period in the church coincided with the broader cultural movement of Enlightenment, during which the rationality of the individual human was vaunted as the most powerful force in the cosmos, and—at least in literature and philosophy—God was dethroned.

But even so, many philosophers retained a sense that they were a part of something bigger than themselves, and some turned to the concept of the *sublime* to explore and explain that feeling. That word, which has become a lodestar of my evolving spirituality in the outdoors, refers to something so amazing or beautiful that it inspires awe, thus lending itself to philosophical reflection on nature in its most august and intimidating forms. As early as 1688, English playwright John Dennis described his experience of hiking in the Swiss Alps: "We walk'd upon the very brink, in a literal sense, of Destruction; one Stumble, and both Life and Carcass had been at once destroy'd. The sense of all this produc'd different emotions in me, viz. *a delightful Horrour, a terrible Joy,* and at the same time, that I was infinitely, pleas'd I trembled."[4]

The following century, Edmund Burke, reflecting on this delightful terror, wrote that the sublime is "productive of the strongest emotion which the mind is capable of feeling."[5] Romantic artists in Europe and the United States painted majestic nature scenes: massive mountain peaks dwarfing the human figures in the foreground, towering waves about to consume a ship full of frightened sailors. Nature is terrifying and demands our awe, our reverence, these paintings announce.

Then Immanuel Kant, the philosophical giant of the eighteenth century, turned his attention to the sublime. When we're confronted with the immensity of nature and its inherent danger to us, we're overwhelmed, Kant writes; we're reminded of our fragility:

> Bold, overhanging, and, as it were, threatening rocks, thunderclouds piled up the vault of heaven, borne along with flashes and peals, volcanoes in all their violence of destruction, hurricanes leaving desolation in their track, the boundless ocean rising with rebellious force, the high waterfall of some mighty river, and the like, make our power of resistance of trifling moment in comparison with their might.[6]

This—the sublime—is why I venture into wild places. Because, as Kant goes on to write, when we're confronted with nature's danger, its ability to snuff us out, we're reminded that we are part of something bigger than ourselves. But we're not doomed and should not despair, Kant exhorts, because when we confront that danger and step into it, we embrace our agency as free and independent beings. It's what makes us fully human.

"In the woods, we return to reason and faith," wrote Ralph Waldo Emerson, the American transcendentalist. Like a snake sloughing off its skin, adults become children in the wild; the woods minister to us by laying bare the "occult relation between man and the vegetable." Rapturously, he writes of a moment in the wilderness: "Standing on the bare ground,—my head bathed by the blithe air, and uplifted into infinite space,—all mean egotism vanishes. I become a transparent eyeball; I am nothing; I see all; the currents of the Universal Being circulate through me; I am part or particle of God."[7] I've felt this, too: both part of the force that created the cosmos, and tiny mite of nothingness in comparison to the billions upon billions of galaxies swirling across the cosmos. Other aspects of human experience may bring us into contact with the sublime, but nothing does it like the wilderness.

Wild places make demands on us: that we have courage and smarts, that we work with nature rather than against it, that we keep our wits about us. That we learn the ways of the woods and plains and deserts and mountains; that we not allow our modern sensibilities to make us squeamish to the savagery of the predator-prey relationship.

That we face our own mortality.

I've immersed myself in the sublime, wrapped myself in the vestments of the natural world, by walking out of the church and into the woods, and that journey saved me. What follows are the lessons I've learned in the wilderness, and from the God who dwells there, the God who meets us in the wild places.

2

Peace

Travel by canoe is not a necessity, and will nevermore be the most efficient way to get from one region to another, or even from one lake to another—anywhere. A canoe trip has become simply a rite of oneness with certain terrain, a diversion of the field, an act performed not because it is necessary but because there is value in the act itself.

—John McPhee, *The Survival of the Bark Canoe*

DEEP IN THE MYTHIC JUMBLE OF WATER AND ISLANDS THAT IS LAKE of the Woods, Doug and I sit in his duck boat awaiting dawn. Loons call back and forth from distant bays, their cries mixed with the hum of mosquitoes. We'd risen at 3:30 a.m., grabbed a thermos of coffee, and set out in the duck boat for our morning commute through a labyrinth of channels and open water guided only by blinking buoy lights and Doug's memory.

In the North Country, a moonless night means deep darkness. From our boat, we can see a net of stars stretched across the sky, the aurora borealis swirling before us as we motor north. Doug sits on the back bench of the boat, manning the 40-horsepower outboard motor—a smaller just-in-case outboard is also clamped to the transom; both are painted camouflage. My spot on the middle bench is spine-crushingly bouncy, so I slide down to the deck and sit on a flotation cushion, wedging another cushion between my back and the metal seat-edge behind me. I drape my legs over a bag of decoys, and Doug's dogs nestle in on either side of me.

Doug does not yet have the handheld GPS device that he will on our later hunts; he doesn't even have a map. The blinking beacons provide guidance for a clear passage, but they also require navigation that is treacherous during high winds because they force us to move through open water rather than hewing closer to shore with its calmer water. Doug captains the boat by feel and memory. I hold a million-candle-watt spotlight, powered by a car battery. We don't talk during the boat rides, for several reasons: the noise of the outboard; we're facing the same direction; and Doug has to concentrate completely on the path ahead of us. Hurtling into the dark at 15 knots, low-level dread emanates from somewhere behind my sternum. Once every few minutes, Doug shouts at me to shine the light at 11 o'clock or 2 o'clock—the bow of the boat representing high noon. He's instructed me to flash it for just a split second, enough for him to calibrate how far we are from shore, but not long enough to wash out his night vision.

Every island looks the same. We've traveled for 30 or 45 minutes, and I've flashed a million candles worth of light at the shore on one side of us or the other a dozen times, illuminating rocks and trees, rocks and trees, rocks and trees. Not a single unique landmark. Just rocks and trees. And yet somehow, in the dark, without a map, Doug skirts this island and turns down that channel and comes about around another promontory and we end up, at the end of a two-hour ride, in a cove full of wild rice.

Arriving at Seemo Bay, hard into the Canadian shield, we toss decoys into the water and Doug guns the motor, launching the boat onto a bog. Now we wait.

On cue, songbirds begin their trills and crows their caws. Enough light wraps around the horizon from the approaching sun that we catch a glimpse of a moose, chest deep in water and muck, dining on aquatic vegetation.

One of the most thrilling experiences of hunting is hearing the whistle of wings overhead, the *wooooosh* of a bird landing in the water, and the chuckle-quacks of ducks feeding, all while wrapped in the gray blanket of pre-dawn, waiting for the sun to pull back the covers and reveal—what? Ten ducks on the water? A hundred?

The sky brightens slowly. Like the point-of-view shot of a character in a movie coming out of a coma, the world gradually comes into focus. Cattails curtain me off from the water and the waterfowl. I await Doug's command. Then, thirty minutes before sunrise, he whispers, "Okay!" and we stand. Ducks explode from the water in a flurry of wings and feet; we each blast three times, emptying our guns, and the dogs burst from the boat. The previous two-and-a-half hours of preparation culminate in five seconds of joyous pandemonium. The dogs return with a couple of ducks we've managed to shoot.

After the initial barrage of gunfire, we settle in to wait on more ducks, and they appear in twos and fours over the next couple hours. As a novice hunter, I am a terrible shot, but Doug rarely misses. He barks at me not to so much as blink when ducks overfly us, but I find it impossible and steal glances skyward. Off the birds wing, spooked by my movement, and Doug grunts his displeasure.

Dallas, a sleek, muscular, and blockheaded dog, bolts early on a missed shot. Doug screams at him to return to the boat, hauling the dripping dog over the gunnel. Frantically looking around the boat, he grabs our plastic coffee thermos and smashes it over the dog's head. Shards of the glass tube liner shimmer on the bottom of the boat, and Dallas, coffee streaming down his black coat, looks at Doug expectantly, waiting to be rewarded for something or other. The dog is none the worse for wear. "Well, there goes our morning coffee," Doug says, laughing.

When the ducks stop flying, it's time to pull down the camo screens we'd erected and shove the boat off the bog to retrieve our decoys. I struggle with a push-pole against the sludge, but the boat will not budge. Then I hear splashing in the water behind me. Doug has disrobed and climbed out. Naked, belly-deep in smelly muck, he pushes the boat, a foot at a time, until it slides free of the bog. Then he heaves himself back over the side, 270 pounds, six-foot-four-inches of flesh, flopping on the boat bottom like a trophy fish that no one wants to catch.

No matter how cold and stormy the journey to our morning hunting spot, the ride back to the cabin is always warm and delightful, at least in my memory. I drop into my spot between wet decoys and wet dogs and close my eyes, the autumnal sun warm on my face as we motor south; the drone of the engine lulls me in and out of sleep. I am as far away from my troubled marriage, from my anger, anxiety, and despair as I can imagine—I don't have kids yet, making it easier to lose myself in the wilderness.

Back at the cabin, Doug sits in a chair; I stand with my back to him and his foot between my legs and I pull off his rubber boots, which are too tight for his feet. We eat a massive breakfast and then nap for hours. Upon waking, we eat again and prep for the evening hunt. Doug teaches me how to clean my shotgun. Since I have no waders, he shows me how duct-taping the tops of my boots to my pants will keep water out.

We get crossways at times. I pull a chair around to the south side of the cabin so that I can catch some afternoon sun and look out over the lake as I pluck ducks. When Doug finds me, ankle-deep in feathers, he grows angry, asking why I would do that here. I'm confused. We're in the middle of nowhere. Why does he care if duck feathers collect around the cabin? They'll all blow away in the next storm. He tells me that his dad wouldn't like it, that I should find another place to do it. Most odd about this exchange is that Doug's ailing father lives in Florida, hasn't been to the cabin in years, and will never visit the cabin again.

As I dice tomatoes for a salad, Doug looks over my shoulder and tells me a better way to hold the knife. "You're not my father!" I scream with some Freudian rage that was hidden in the depths of my soul, storming off to my bedroom, slamming the door, and melodramatically throwing myself on the bed. (To this day, Doug and I laugh about that incident, but my laughter is disingenuous—I remain troubled by that outburst and its source.)

But mainly, days at Whit's End are joyous. We play cards and talk about Jesus and the Bible. Every once in a while, Doug hears something wonky from the generator that powers the cabin, and he explodes through the screen door in nothing but boxer shorts, sprinting around back, sure that the engine has run out of oil and is going to seize up and die. He saunters back to the cabin, his big belly heaving for breath, and declares the crisis averted.

"Nothing motivates like irrational fear!" he proclaims.

We leave for the evening hunt around 4 p.m., the inverse of the morning hunt: the journey out is pleasant, the journey home harrowing. Finding our preferred bay, we cast decoys and hide ourselves and the boat. Ducks looking for a safe and secluded spot for the night cup their wings upon seeing their plastic compatriots and hearing Doug's quacking on his duck call—he asks me not to blow mine. We shoot some. Then, after sunset, we retrieve the decoys by the light of the spotlight and start the journey home.

The weather has turned sour, making the hunting good and the boating bad. As the craft slips out of Dawson Bay and into open water, fog settles in, combined with snow and wind and darkness. With three- and four-foot breakers on the lake, Doug guides the duck boat close to shore, which affords us some shelter from the wind. Nevertheless, waves occasionally creep over the gunwales and onto my lap. Snow flies horizontally, and when I flash the spotlight toward shore to give Doug a bearing, we see nothing but white streaks of snow against the fog, forming an overexposed image on my retinas that I try to blink away.

I am cold—maybe the coldest I've ever been. In spite of the many layers of cotton and rubber and neoprene that wrap me like a burrito, the wind sneaks in through sleeve holes and zipper lines. Sleet pelts my face, melts, and drips down my neck. I shiver uncontrollably, wracking my body. I withdraw my fingers from their slots in my gloves; I pull my arms in from the sleeves of my coat and clutch my torso. Finally I acquiesce: I am going to be cold, and nothing can be done about it. There is no escape from the cold. I need to accept it.

Doug tells me to leave the lamp on and shine it downward, at the shore, where the water meets the land. We slowly motor on. Waves clap at the port side of the boat like Neptune is hitting it with a baseball bat, and Doug struggles to keep the shoreline within a few feet of our starboard side. He's trimmed the outboard to a speed fast enough to keep us moving forward, but slow enough that if we hit a big rock we probably won't capsize.

I don't yet know that we are lost.

After about an hour-and-a-half, Doug steers the boat into a se-cluded bay and tells me. He took a wrong turn around one of the myriad islands that all look the same. He admits that he can't distin-guish his normal points of navigation through the fog and snow. He says that we're running low on gas for the motor. He tells me that at some point, we'll have to pull up on shore and spend the night on an island, hopefully with enough fuel still in the tank to get us back to the cabin in the morning from wherever we are.

He flips the lever on the motor from idle to forward and swings the boat out of the placid bay and back into the storm, in the direction that he thinks we should probably be going.

I settle back into my spot between dogs and decoys and perform my spotlight duty.

I take an inner audit of myself. I should feel cold and scared, but instead I feel warm and safe. This is surely the most physical peril I've been in, I think. We're in danger of spending the night exposed as tem-peratures drop, with no food, no fuel for the boat, and no one having any idea where we are. And yet I am exceptionally calm. I don't un-derstand it myself, being that my inner peace is so at odds with our circumstances.

My audit reveals a few truths. For one, I can do nothing to improve our situation. I cannot create more gasoline, nor can I determine where we are. I cannot change the weather or communicate our position to loved ones. I can't conjure food and water out of thin air or start a fire with the wave of my hand. I am helpless.

I realize that I have been completely and totally reliant upon Doug for everything all week. I could not have managed a single aspect of this trip on my own. I've had to trust Doug. What good will it do me to stop trusting him now? Either he's capable of pulling us out of this predicament, or he's not. My fate is in his hands.

So I sit back. I don't pray and I don't hope. I don't panic, either. I settle into a calm so deep that I've often longed to return to that boat on that stormy night, just to access that peace again.

Churches are sometime oxymoronically named. When I was growing up, a congregation named "Grace Church" was known to produce some of the most judgmental Christians in our town. And another that goes by the moniker "Peace" suffered through several internal civil wars over the years, ultimately divorcing from their denomination over gay marriage.

Peace is easier to claim than it is to achieve. When I was a pastor, if you would have asked me the most important characteristic of the Christian life, I would have responded unequivocally: peace. I would have told you that we are a people of peace who follow the Prince of Peace, that Jesus blessed the peacemakers and Paul said that the reason Jesus came was to make peace between God and us.

I preached peace, but my life was anything but peaceful. I had constant conflict at home, strife I carried with me to church. And, if that weren't enough, I was making a name for myself as a top Christian blogger by picking fights on the internet—if I wrote a post criticizing another preacher or theologian, my numbers jumped; the meaner I was, the more traffic I got, and I leaned into that formula because it fed my ego—another mask to hide the deeper anxiety about my self-worth. Each of those environs—at home, at work, online—brought out the worst in me; they preyed on my deepest insecurities, and I responded with aggressive defensiveness. I didn't bring peace, I brought war.

I think I have such a vivid memory of the stormy night in the duck boat because of the peace I felt. The calm. The warmth. Everything I'd ever wanted from Jesus was actuated with Doug, this big, blundering, bombastic hunting mentor of mine. Doug's competence affected me. If he can't get us out of this, I figured, no one can.

He did get us out. At some point in the night, he either figured out where we were or stumbled upon a familiar landmark; he fixed our position on a point on the map in his mind, and he navigated us home. We puttered up to the dock on fumes. The dogs gleefully jumped out of the boat and sprinted up to the cabin door, with Doug and me on their heels. Never has a belly full of spaghetti and a saggy twin mattress felt so good.

(Doug was not so lucky the next fall, when his boat capsized and sank on a similarly stormy night. He and his hunting buddy swam to shore and spent a frigid night huddled together with the dogs before having to swim across to Whit's End the next day. Then, having eaten a box of mouse poison, one of Doug's dogs died in his arms.)

Doug doesn't own Whit's End anymore. His father died, and his brother succumbed to alcoholism a couple years after that. Doug's own health deteriorated, with joint problems and a litany of ankle and foot surgeries that have left him semi-crippled. He hadn't been to the cabin in years. He told me that the roof over the back bedroom, where I used to stay, collapsed. He ultimately sold what was left of it.

"What about the decoys and duck boats?" I asked.

"Sold it all," he said. "Lock, stock, and barrel."

I only hunted there with Doug three times, and I miss it. Now I'm the guy teaching someone else to hunt—how to clean a gun, train a dog, sit still in a blind. But I miss the freedom that came with the complete lack of responsibility. All I needed to do on those hunts was whatever Doug told me to do. When I thought for myself, I got into trouble, but when I did what he said, everything was fine. Plus, the anger that so vexed me at home and church and online faded when I was at his cabin, like the morning fog burned off by the piercing northern sun.

At the time, I didn't know why I wanted to learn hunting from Doug—if I did reflect on it, I suppose I chalked it up to some masculine impulse, or simply a desire for a new hobby. But looking back, the ineluctable truth is this: I needed an escape, one that brought me some peace. In spite of my unwillingness to admit it, my failing marriage clawed at my soul, leaving it shredded and bleeding. And my faith, mediated by the organized religion that paid my salary, was a façade—a grand-looking building on the outside, falsely fronting little more than a dark closet.

But that night on Lake of the Woods, I put my faith not in an institution or a doctrine—I put it in a *person* who sat behind me and helmed the boat. As a proxy for God, Doug was full of foibles and imperfections. But he was *real*, as was the terrifyingly sublime wilderness that enveloped us. God visited me in Doug. Paradoxically, in the midst of an exploit that involves gunshots and death, I felt something I'd been promised in church: peace that surpasses all understanding.

Sigurd Olson is a hero of mine. When I guide canoe trips, I require everyone on the trip to read a book of his as a prerequisite. And on the trip, I insist that they refer to him as St. Sigurd.

Olson was born in Chicago in 1899 and grew up in northern Wisconsin, the son of pious Swedes. He studied biology in college and then took a job teaching the subject at Ely Junior College in northern Minnesota. But what really set the trajectory for his life was a canoe trip he took at age 22 through the lakes on the border between Minnesota and Canada.

In 1947 he left his teaching post and spent the rest of his life, until his death in 1982, writing and advocating for protection of the wilderness, particularly those border lakes he loved so much. He served as president of the Wilderness Society, consulted with the Secretary of the Interior, testified before Congress, and had a role in the establishment of Voyageurs National Park, the Arctic National Wildlife Refuge, and, of course, the Boundary Waters Canoe Area Wilderness (BWCA).

But what most interests me about Olson is *why* he worked so hard to preserve wild places. When you read his books and speeches, it's clear: he worried that modern life was squeezing the peace and tranquility out of our lives, and that only wild places can save us. In a speech to the Sierra Club's Wilderness Conference in 1965, he traced the history of humankind, arguing that for millennia, our way of life had barely changed. Then, dramatically, in the early twentieth century, we were "hurled into a machine age of whirring speed and complexity where the ancient ecological and emotional balances were upset."

While our surroundings have changed, our spiritual longings have not. We still desire solitude, tranquility, and places where we can escape the whir of modernity. "Companionship with the gods and true leisure," he said, is why we still seek wild places, because when we are communing with our gods—whoever those gods may be—we can "forget the problems and petty distractions of the workaday world and reach out to spiritual realizations that renew [us]."

Starkly put, there are more of us on the planet every year, and less wild places. Yet we need the wilderness to meet our most primitive and enduring spiritual needs: remembering who we are, reconnecting us with the rest of creation and with the One who created it all. What little wilderness remains, we must save: "We live close to the last wilderness lake country in the middle west, a country of lakes and rivers and forests that for beauty and charm have no counterpart. Here is an island of solitude, a bit of eternity, where men may always come to refresh their souls and to know peace."[1]

The BWCA that St. Sigurd helped establish sits on the limen between Minnesota and Canada, a million acres, no motors allowed. I go there every year.

A few years back, paddling with a small group of guys, we traversed a dozen lakes on a five-day paddle-and-portage journey off the end of the Gunflint Trail. On the second day, we'd made it through Ester and Hanson Lakes and decamped on a promontory on the South Arm of Big Knife Lake. The day was hot—too hot for September—and after setting up camp we paddled to a nearby waterfall and took turns letting the cold downpour wash over us. Back at camp a less welcome downpour greeted us just as we were cooking dinner, and we joked that the smallmouth bass on the fire went from grilled to poached as the Bethany skillet filled with rainwater. The fish tasted great nonetheless.

Everyone went to bed early and damp, and I rolled around restlessly. Wide awake at 3 a.m., I pulled my sleeping bag and a camp chair from the tent, zipped the flap closed behind me, and walked by the light of my headlamp to a piece of granite the size of a small house that jutted out over the lake. I slid back into my bag and pulled the drawstring tight, then I awkwardly dropped into the chair, cocooned in the bag.

The rain had stopped, the sky had cleared, and the temperature had dropped. I looked out over the lake. The quarter moon had already set, revealing a billion stars. Unlike so many calm summer nights in the north, on this night a steady wind blew. The granite jetty on which I sat pointed directly into the southwesterly breeze. Waves splashed on the rocks below me. As if on cue, loons called back-and-forth from one distant bay to another.

If I had to guess, I'd say the wind that night was blowing at 10 to 15 miles per hour. But I'd rather not guess. I'd rather just say that the wind blew at just the right force, strong enough to keep the late hatch mosquitoes at bay, but not strong enough to chase me back to the tent. Nine hours earlier, the dinner downpour washed the hot, humid air out of lake country, and behind it swept an all-night zephyr, pushing out the last remnants of summer, with autumn in tow.

Although half-a-dozen men slept in tents 50 yards away, I was alone. I braced for loneliness because that's what I'd felt for so many years whenever I was alone—which is why I assiduously avoided being alone. I peered into the center of the Milky Way, tracked the occasional satellite, and nodded in and out of sleep.

And I did not feel lonely.

Instead, I received an epiphany of peace.

For so long, I had feared loneliness, and to stave it off I sacrificed peace. My 20s was a series of intense romantic relationships, culminating in my first marriage. I just wanted to escape the loneliness. I feared the silence and embraced the noise, regardless of the cost.

The cost, it turned out, was extraordinary.

But now, 20 years later, I was okay. I was at peace.

While I'd had moments of joy, even exhilaration—finding love again and marrying Courtney, cheering my kids' achievements—I had not found peace. I surrounded myself with busyness, drowning out the silence that might remind me of my pain, might make me look Narcissus in the eye—he's the monster under my bed.

The truth is, I'd never experienced much peace—the night in Doug's boat was a notable exception. I'd lived for a long time under the illusion that peace was just around the next corner. If I could just fix my marriage or get out of it or win custody or get a big-enough book deal, my soul would stop spinning like a top, I could cease my striving.

But I ignored the wisdom of every spiritual tradition: peace comes from within. On that night in the BWCA, I experienced the soul-penetrating peace that I had not felt since the night in Doug's boat. She came not as a visitor from outside me, an alternative to the monster beneath my bed, but from within me. Only in the transcendent quiet of a northern lake could I lower the mask and let her in—let her heal that deeper anxiety about my own self-worth.

I needed to learn that lesson for myself, I suppose, but I was never going to learn it while rushing around in my day-to-day life. I needed to come out here, where the tentacles of data could not reach me. I'd retrograded to pure analog, just me and the lake and the loons.

Christians in the West—those of us who grew up Catholic or Protestant—tend to think of God as an external being, outside of us and sovereign over us. Our liturgies and hymns reflect that idea of God, and even our body language does—just think of an athlete pointing to the sky after scoring, giving credit to God, who is up there, not down here. But Eastern Christians—mostly known as Orthodox—have another idea, for which they use the Greek word *theosis*.

Theosis is the belief that human beings can, through a spiritual process, achieve union with God, even partaking in God's unique divine nature—alternative names for theosis include *deification* and *divinization*. That concept would be anathema to most theologians in the Western tradition, but Eastern Christians take seriously the biblical assurances that the Spirit of God dwells within each of us.

Think of it like a small, glowing ember, deep within us, within every person. If we get it some oxygen, it will grow to a flame; feed it some wood and it'll soon be a roaring fire. The *Philokalia*, a book of Orthodox wisdom, contains this gem:

> Abba Lot went to see Abba Joseph and said to him, "Abba, as far as I can, I do my little office, I read my psalms, I fast a little bit, I pray and I meditate, I live in peace with others as far as I can, I purify my thoughts. Tell me, Father, what else, what more can I do?" Then the old man, Abba Joseph, stood up, stretched out his hands toward heaven, and his fingers became like ten lamps of fire, and he said to him, "If you will, you can become all flame."[2]

Abbas Lot and Joseph lived in fifth century Egypt, part of a group we now call the Desert Fathers and Mothers. Whereas in the West, monks and nuns lived together in communities, the abbas and ammas of the East tended toward solitude, often living in caves for extended periods of time. They sought wild places so they could stoke that internal fire.

Another monk, Evagrius the Solitary, fled Constantinople and its temptations in the 380s and settled in the desert. The *Philokalia* quotes him:

> I urge you to welcome exile. It frees you from all the entanglements of your own locality, and allows you to enjoy the blessings of stillness undistracted. Do not stay in a town, but persevere in the wilderness. "Lo," says the Psalm, "then would I wander far off, and remain in the wilderness" (Ps. 55:7). If possible, do not visit a town at all. For you will find there nothing of benefit, nothing useful, nothing profitable for your way of life. To quote the Psalm again, "I have seen violence and strife in the city" (Ps. 55:9). So seek out places that are free from distraction, and solitary.[3]

The Egyptian wilderness was not without risk. The abbas and ammas were attacked by creatures both physical and spiritual. But because they'd fanned that divine flame within themselves, they experienced peace in the midst of assault. "The experienced have the best teacher of all," said Hesychios the Priest, deep in the Sinai wilderness: "The activity, discernment, and peace of God."[4]

I grew up in the Reformed version of Christianity, where, according to the Presbyterian Book of Order, worship is to take place "decently and in order." Everything in the sanctuary of my youth was at right angles, and when we walked into the service on Sunday we knew what we were going to get, because it was invariably the same as the previous Sunday.

Wilderness, by contrast, is disorderly and chaotic, even violent. It's paradoxical, seeking peace in wild places, but most spiritual truths are paradoxical.

When I walk into the woods, I don't know what I'm going to get. Even if I'm traveling a path that I've trod many times before, I'm likely to face new obstacles, confront new challenges, and meet new travelers—human and non-human—along the way. The path itself may

have changed, affected by forces larger than me. Other than the introduction of video screens, the sanctuary of my former church looks the
same as it did when I was in ninth grade. But every one of the portages
I walked on my first trip to the BWCA that same year has evolved with
new vegetation and toppled trees, erosion and moose tracks. The woods
are ever-changing.

After decades away from the Boundary Waters, I'd become one of
the many Minnesotans who say, "I love the Boundary Waters. I went
there as a kid. But I haven't been back in a long time. Maybe next
year. . . ." Year after year I said this. Until I finally went, and it was even
better than I remembered. So I made a commitment: I am going to
visit the BWCA at least once a year as long as I'm physically able.

Years ago, someone taught me to stop my car a block or two after
I've left my house for a canoe trip, open the door, and let everything
that might keep me from peace symbolically pour out of the car and
down the drain. It's my way of leaving the anxieties of my everyday life
behind so that I can walk into the wild free of those burdens.

At the launch site, before I push my canoe into the water, I take a
moment to set an intention for the trip, to focus my energy on what's
ahead. Anxiety is inevitable—I feel it, though I've stood here many
times before. I pay attention to that anxiety: it's an evolutionary trait
meant to keep me alive.

Then the canoe slides into the lake. Invariably, when I'm guiding
a trip, the group is chatty on the first day, the excitement of the launch
mixing with the social awkwardness of getting to know one another.
One route that I often choose starts in a channel that has cabins on
either side. The farther north we paddle, the less frequent the buildings,
until we swing past Munker Island into the expanse of Lake Saganaga.
That transition, from the narrows to open water, tends to take novice
paddlers by surprise, so it's about then that I suggest that we journey
in silence for the next hour. That's more of a challenge for some than
others, but we do it each day, paddling for a few miles in silence. When
you stop listening for the voices of your fellow humans, you tend to be
more attentive to other sounds: water lapping at the kevlar canoe, a
paddle swishing through water, wind in the jack pines, a beaver slap-
ping its tail.

It usually takes me a day or two to access true inner peace in the wilderness. Like tapping maple trees, the sap is in there, but the temperature needs to be just right for it to run down the spout and into the bucket. And that's a big part of it: remembering that the peace doesn't live in the wilderness, waiting for me. I'm bringing the peace with me—it's inside of me. The wilderness is the catalyst, the conduit for the emergence of theosis, blowing on that ember of peace that dwells deeply within me, bringing it to full flame.

The court-appointed psychologist wasn't wrong. I wore masks because I feared what I'd find if I looked deep within—masks of aggression and strength and disputation to hide what I assumed was an inner emptiness. But those masks serve no purpose in the middle of nowhere, so I can let them fall away. And what dwells within me is a little flame. It just needs the breeze off a northern lake to bring it to life.

3

Place

No one yet has made a list of places where the extraordinary may happen and where it may not. Still, there are indications. Among crowds, in drawing rooms, among easements and comforts and pleasures, it is seldom seen. It likes the out-of-doors.

—Mary Oliver, *Upstream: Selected Essays*

IN THE MIDDLE AGES, EVERY CHRISTIAN IN EUROPE WHO WAS physically able was expected to make a pilgrimage. The journey itself was penance, the pilgrims shriven of their sins as they made their way toward Jerusalem, Rome, or Santiago. To this day, tens of thousands of pilgrims walk the *Peregrinatio Compostellana* annually, just as millions of Muslims make the Hajj to Mecca.

Our family lake cabin in Central Minnesota is 127 miles from our home in the suburbs, on land that's been in the family for three generations. The drive takes anywhere from two hours to three-plus if I make the mistake of driving north on the Friday afternoon of a holiday weekend. While it may not cleanse me of my sins, the drive does transport me, preparing me to enter the north woods. I know every Dairy Queen and knick-knack spot along the way. I've watched businesses open, sputter, and close; I've witnessed the proliferation of car dealerships around Zimmerman and cursed the three stoplights in Elk River. I've watched abandoned barns slowly lean, lean, lean—and then collapse.

I'm a lot more at peace with the drive than I used to be. I now consider it an indispensable part of the weekend—a mini-pilgrimage.

The planning for a summer weekend begins on Monday or Tuesday. The bigger the group, the more sophisticated the preparation. We can sleep 16—more if couples share beds. Someone creates a Google Doc and shares it with the group. We negotiate sleeping arrangements, and we sign up for meals, appetizers, and beverages. We check in with the family members who went up last weekend: Is there milk in the fridge? Do we have enough charcoal? How much gas is in the boats?

Cars arrive. Children burst from their carseats like criminals sprung from prison. Dogs leap out of hatchbacks and tear around with joy untold, peeing on all the old spots. Adults haul coolers into the kitchen and load the fridge. Someone hands me a beer. The kids already have their swimsuits on and they're begging us to take them tubing. Give us a minute, we tell them.

We've upgraded the place in the decades since my grandfather, who built the cabin, died. In addition to the washer and dryer, we've got a dishwasher and wifi. But it's still rustic—definitely a cabin, not a lake home. Neither the main room in the cabin nor the kitchen can handle as many people as we can sleep, so we're constantly shooing kids outside.

My kids are the oldest among the grandchildren, in high school and college. Aidan will take out the fishing boat for hours at a time, occasionally texting me photos of largemouth bass that he's caught-and-released. Tanner and Lily, home from college, seem to use our weekends at the cabin primarily as a time to catch up on sleep. I can't blame them, since I sleep better at the cabin than I do at home, especially when we have "good sleeping weather," as my dad used to say.

The younger kids are slathered with sunscreen and sent down the switchback trail to the lake. We strip off boat covers and pull tubes and noodles out of the lakeside shed. Out come paddleboards and the Lilypad, a floating foam island. We crack another beer and sit at the end of the dock, watching the kids play King of the Hill on the diving raft and listening to their jubilant screams.

Here in the North, the sun sticks around until after 9 p.m. on summer nights, and our internal clocks shift with it. We're in no rush. Around 6, someone will head back up the hill to the cabin to replenish our beverages and fix a tray of hors d'oeuvres for our nightly cocktail cruise on the pontoon boat. Through years of research, I've determined that 3.5-miles-per-hour is the perfect speed for the voyage. We wave at passing boats and at fellow cabin owners fishing off the ends of their docks. We look for the loons, and if we find them we cut the engine and float and watch them dive and resurface.

Back at the cabin, someone starts the coals—no gas grills allowed. My mother starts a load of dishes, a couple kids are deputized to set the table, while others shower or play ping pong while dinner is prepared. Growing up, we ate lots of burgers and steaks at the cabin, but these days we try to outdo each other with gourmet dishes: someone smoked a pork butt all day, or we're having venison gyros, or there's a turkey on the rotisserie. After dinner, maybe just one more glass of wine out on the deck, with a cigar. Someone comments about the lack (or abundance) of mosquitoes this year, and one-by-one we peel off for bed.

I'm up early the next morning. I fire up the coffeemaker and let the dogs out of the garage while it's brewing. Out on the deck with a cup of coffee and a slice of banana bread and a book—it's the best time of the day, as the woods awaken.

Saturday is for projects. We've got to clean the garage or sharpen chains for the saws. We're building a new canoe rack or planting hundreds of balsam trees. We're grading the driveway or splitting firewood. But by mid-afternoon it's time for a beer and a nap, then it's back down to the lake to repeat the cycle.

Sunday is bittersweet. At some point in the late morning, one family or another starts piling duffels and garbage bags behind their car, the first step toward the inevitable departure. The sound of the vacuum cleaner interrupts our meditations. Rugs are shaken out over the deck. The boats are covered. We lock up, set the alarm, and pull the gate closed behind us as we join the reverse-pilgrimage, the descent from heaven to purgatory.

Before the divorce, my life looked like one of conventional beauty. Our big house in the middle of a quiet, suburban street boasted a giant cottonwood out back that snowed down puffballs every June. Two cars parked in the garage. Kids happily jumping on the trampoline. Hopscotch chalked on the driveway.

But a different reality brewed indoors: our fights were increasing in frequency and intensity. First, insults were hurled, then items: silverware, shoes, a laptop.

Restless nights stretched on for months, and the sleep deprivation whittled away at my senses. Sometimes I'd sneak in a nap on the small couch in my church office, in spite of its wooden armrests and industrial upholstery. At night, I grew desperate for even an hour or two of rest. I slept in my daughter's top bunk, or in the locked car in the garage.

In those days of little sleep, I nevertheless got up early, jolted awake by anxiety. One morning I walked around the house to the backyard to water the lawn. I turned on the spigot, which sent water through the hose to a rotary impact sprinkler—the kind that goes *chick-chick-chick-chickachickachicka*. The pattern wasn't quite right. I walked out into the yard to adjust it. I bent over to turn the small nut that directs the flow, and searing pain knifed through my back, shoving me to the ground. I lay there, prone, for several minutes, getting sprinkled. I tried to stand but collapsed. I army-crawled through the grass, the stream of water showering me every few seconds, in my pajama bottoms and t-shirt, at five in the morning. I got to the back door and reached up for the knob. Locked. I lay there soaking wet for two hours before one of my kids opened the door and let me in.

On a trip to Dublin, my back seized up again. At the transfer in Newark, I couldn't get out of my seat. Agents from Delta Airlines helped me into a wheelchair and rolled me out of the plane. Instead of canceling the speaking engagement and returning home, I flew on to Ireland and suffered through a week of unimaginable pain—better to be in pain and far away than in pain at home.

Back pain wasn't my only problem in those years. At least three times I went to urgent care for abdominal pain that doubled me over. Diagnosis: intestinal distress caused by anxiety. Once I had chest pain that I was sure was cardiac arrest—I sat in the minivan and wondered how I could have a heart attack at age 35. My wife dropped me at the ER, unwilling to walk me inside, so far apart had we grown. My parents came and sat with me. Diagnosis: pericarditis—my heart sac was sick.

My body knew well before my mind did: my life was killing me. Nevertheless, for years I stuck to the script, ignoring the signs that were becoming increasingly clear to everyone around me. I alternated between begging and fleeing. Sometimes I tried to debate us back into a working marriage. Other times I pled. But mostly I fled. I was at a speaking gig in Oregon when Tanner fell and broke his arm, backstage at another gig in Malaysia when I got the call that he'd contracted mononucleosis and was admitted to the hospital. I sat in hotel rooms around the world and cranked out books, authoring one or two per year. Every day I would open my email to find another invitation to speak. My personal and professional lives were moving in opposite directions.

I'd been told by others: once you even mention the word *divorce*, it's inevitable. So I never mentioned it. I did not even consider it. I couldn't do that to the kids—my love for them trumped my own suffering.

I made a sacred vow, I protested when the first of my friends finally had the audacity to suggest that maybe a split would be best for everyone involved, kids included.

I'm not a quitter, I said.

Who ever said marriage was easy? I asked.

But I knew another truth: in my line of work, divorce is a stigma, an unerasable scar, like the holes in Jesus' hands, but without the accompanying salvation. Finally contemplating the split, I sat in my parents' basement at two in the morning, talking on the phone to another cleric who was getting divorced.

"Do you think our careers can survive this?" she asked.

"Yes, definitely," I replied with false confidence, going on to tell her that people just don't care about divorce anymore, even church people. But I didn't believe what I was saying. I knew her suspicions were correct, that to finally concede the inevitability of divorce would likely be the end of my career as a reverend.

I wondered how everything could have gone so wrong. I'd done what I was supposed to, I'd been faithful to God and pursued my vocation with vigor. I forewent opportunity and salary to serve the Lord. I'd done mission work. I held up my end, but now it seemed that God was defaulting on our bargain. I prayed for peace in the marriage and went to couples' therapy and bought flowers and did the little things and the big things, but it just kept unraveling.

When I read the court-ordered psychological report, it wasn't the first time I'd been confronted with my lack of self-worth. As a teenager, I'd often get deliberately lost in the woods at our cabin. I'd walk partway down the mile-long, two-track driveway and then turn north, into the forest, and wander, not sure where I was going or how long I'd be gone. Thoughts not uncommon to a teenage boy troubled me: thoughts of girls and God and college and whether any of my friends really liked me. A creek runs through the woods, and I'd sit next to it, leaning against a tree, alone, no parents surveilling me, enveloped by solitude.

Our family land lies on the liminal thread between deciduous and coniferous biomes. A tornado in 1973 uprooted massive white pines and basswoods, red pines and maples, spruce and oak. Quaking aspen, the opportunist of northern forests, sprung up in their place. My grandfather, who bought the land in 1964, grieved the loss of the majestic pines and considered selling.

But aspen impress in their own way. Each individual aspen tree is genetically identical to all others in its stand—biologists call them *clonal colonies*—because they share a root structure. In fact, that root system *is* the organism, each tree an above-ground iteration thereof, like fingers on a hand, or hair on a head. The Pando aspen stand in Utah is considered both the oldest living organism on the planet (80,000 years) and the largest (106 acres and 66,000 tons).

The durability of aspen stems from their stems: the petiole, which joins leaf to branch, is thin and flat, reducing drag and making the tree less susceptible to blowdowns in storms. Instead of falling over in the wind, aspen quake. Their smooth bark is similarly aerodynamic, and it photosynthesizes sunlight, meaning that aspen thrive, and even grow, in winter while other trees slumber.

After the tornado denuded the forest of towering competitors, aspen took over. And 40 years after that, my brother Ted proposed that we log off some sections of the land to give it a fresh start. Aspen is favored for matches, chopsticks, and paper, its pulp more workable and less flammable than other woods. A representative of a paper mill in

Grand Rapids, Minnesota, paid us a visit and quickly agreed to buy 42 acres worth of lumber. Later that year, two massive and extraordinary machines rolled off trailers and onto our land. From each, an arm extended that clutched a tree, cut it at the bottom, stripped it of branches, and laid it in a pile. In a week, the acreage had been cleared and the timber hauled north. What was left looked barren, a moonscape of detritus and slash, difficult for the mind to comprehend after four decades of forest too thick to see through.

But the forest regenerated at a breathtaking pace. Within a year, new clones sprouted, reaching six, ten, twelve feet high. At least in spots, I've tried to tame the aspen. I've cleared the skid trails left by the logging trucks. It hasn't been easy. Alongside Ted, I've logged hundreds of hours in the woods, cutting back aspen shoots with a brush cutter, spraying herbicide on thistles that seem to grow before my eyes, and raking and shoveling rough spots to smooth them enough for a walkable trail.

Once we rented a Bobcat from the hardware store in nearby Deerwood, and I attempted to cut a path along the lake shore. I handled the machine pretty well, I thought. Then as I was backing up to take a run at a tree stump, I rolled up on another stump. Before I could reverse course, momentum and gravity took over. The Bobcat came to rest on its side, me trapped within its protective cage. My dad shook his head, disgusted. "I knew this would happen," he said, and hobbled away on his cane. He was a hard man to impress, and he was particularly critical of me. But a note we found on his desk after his death revealed a deeper truth: like me, he suffered from a profound lack of self-worth, which he masked with anger and impetuousness, both of which he aimed at me when I toppled the Bobcat.

We were in the middle of the woods, so no way could we get a truck in there to right the machine. We tried to tip it up, but it wouldn't budge. We cut down four medium-sized trees and used them as levers, putting our shoulders under them and driving them up. The Bobcat budged, but not enough to tip it. The toxic-yet-intoxicating stink of gasoline, dripping from the upside-down tank, filled our noses.

Then my dad reappeared with a portable winch he'd excavated from some hidden corner of the garage, an implement only he knew we owned. We bolted the winch around a tree uphill from the Bobcat, wrapped the hook around the upper beam of the cage, and started to crank. Slowly, and with some help from the tree-levers, the Bobcat landed aright on its four wheels. Shaken, I drove it out of the woods, onto the trailer, and back to the hardware store. The guy there asked how we could have used a whole tank of fuel when we only ran the unit for two hours. I said I had no idea. He said he'd have to charge me an extra $17 to cover the gas. I said fine. After that I hired a local guy to clear the trails.

In September and October, I walk these trails, a 12-gauge over-under in my hands and dogs quartering in front of me, hunting for ruffed grouse, the most tasty and most wary of game birds. More often than not, I won't see a grouse but will instead hear one explode—that's the best way to describe what it sounds like when in an otherwise quiet woods, a grouse takes off—and never see it as it jets through the forest to safety.

I leave the cabin, walking down the rocky driveway as it skirts the swamp. I cross the gently flowing Nokasippi (Ojibwe for "Tender River") over the culvert into a grove of white pines that escaped the tornado's wrath. The road here is a soft bed of rust-colored needles.

The road rises and I pass under the power lines, a cut through the forest maintained by Crow Wing Power that doubles as a nice shooting lane for turkey and deer. The cut also demarcates the boundary between our property and the Johnson farm. My grandfather didn't get along with Old Man Johnson, but I've mended fences with his son, Todd. Last year I helped him field-dress a buck he shot on opening morning of firearms deer season. He and his son came over for a beer later that day.

I turn right, onto a trail we call the Tornado Road, blazed in 1973 as a temporary driveway when the main road was impassable. The Tornado Road runs parallel to the power line cut and then turns east at the Johnson's corn field, running alongside the field out to the highway. We may bump a grouse in here, but it's unlikely since birch and bass-wood dominate this section of forest and grouse prefer aspen. I pass the tree stand from which Aidan shot his first deer and the spot where I'll set up for turkey next spring. The trail is rough. If I don't work on this trail next spring, the forest will reclaim it. The forest wants all the trails back.

The dogs and I cross the highway and enter a section of young aspen. Before it was logged off, we rarely visited this part of the land, divorced from the rest of our land by Crow Wing County Road 8. A turkey roosts in one of the few remaining white pines, overlooking a deep gulley that in July is bountiful with wild strawberries and must be a bug banquet for the old tom. A grouse flushes and I see only a blurry whiz; I don't even have time to shoulder my gun. The dogs don't give up so easily, tearing off into the woods on a fruitless search for the long-gone bird.

We cross back over the highway and into the thickest stretch of aspen clones where we find the trail I've worked hardest to keep open. This scrubby forest is not beautiful in any conventional sense. Roots and stumps threaten to twist my ankles, and burrs clutch at the dogs' fur. Thistles scratch at my pant legs.

I stop walking, letting the dogs gallop into the scrub to flush whatever they find. There's an unconventional beauty here. The aspen grow under my feet, under the trail that I fight to keep open, under the highway. This organism surrounds me. There's no quit in this aspen. I admire its determination, its resolve. It won't stop growing.

My grandfather bought this land in 1964.

Kicked out of the house upon high school graduation by his itinerant father (the poet laureate of Illinois!), Wright Bower Hawthorne stayed in Minneapolis when his family fled debt collectors to Omaha, and he must have cringed when his father's poem, "Father and Son," ran in the newspaper there:

> Not father and son in a stern, solemn way,
> But chums and good partners at work or at play!
> Not Father and Son separated by fear,
> But comrades in friendship and honor and cheer!

Bower disliked his father, and he despised his stepmother, so he shed no tears when they left. In Minneapolis, he made a name for himself. After one semester at the University of Minnesota, he dropped out and took a job at the Minneapolis *Tribune* as a copyboy. He never worked anywhere else, eventually ascending to executive editor of the newspaper.

Bower was a hard man. Driven and accomplished, he demanded much from his four daughters. But he also loved them fiercely, along with his always-laughing-and-somewhat-scattered wife, Jane. In the summers, he'd rent a cabin for a fortnight at a resort on Clearwater Lake in Crow Wing County. He'd drive the family up, set them up in a small cottage, and drive back to Minneapolis for work. He joined his wife and girls for the second week, during which he'd fish, grill hamburgers, and chain smoke.

Because he couldn't sit still even on vacation, Bower made the rounds. In Minneapolis he palled around with Hubert Humphrey and Walter Mondale, but up north he settled for drinks with Brainerd Mayor Tom O'Brien, an affable fellow, the spitting image of Jimmy Durante, right down to the gin-blossom nose.

O'Brien had a lead on some land on a nearby lake—affordable, he said, because the shoreline was nearly inaccessible, a mile from the highway through thick forest. But Bower loved a deal. He bought 162 acres four years before I was born and began cutting a mile-long road from County Road 8 through the pines, around a cattail slough, over the Nokasippi, and up to a notch between two bluffs overlooking Eagle Lake.

In that cleft, he and a local craftsman raised a small cabin, rough pine walls inside, cedar shakes outside. He split field stones for the chimney and hammered wood pegs in the floorboard, because nails just wouldn't do. The cabin had three rooms: a bedroom, occupied exclusively by Bower and Jane; a main room, with a fireplace and a Hide-a-Bed sofa; and a small kitchen with a hot plate and sink. Through the pipes flowed water pumped up from the lake; an olive green five-gallon jug of drinking water, hauled up in the back of the station wagon, sat on the counter.

My parents often told the story of their honeymoon on the land. My dad's parents gave them a brand new 1965 Ford Mustang, maroon with a black vinyl top. My mom's parents gave them a week at the new cabin, a gift beyond value since Bower didn't allow anyone to stay there without his supervision. The young couple arrived, excited. They opened a cupboard to put up groceries for the week, and thousands of carpenter ants spilled out. Same in the next cupboard, and the next. They spent the first full day of their marriage scooping shovelfuls of ants into a crackling fire.

By 1973, two more cabins had been built: a guest cabin on the bluff to the north, and a bunkhouse, set on top of a small garage that had been cut into the hill. On June 25 of that year, Bower and Jane sat at the lacquered pine table, eating supper. They'd stayed up north through Monday to enjoy the quiet and avoid the back-to-the-cities traffic of Sunday afternoon. They planned to finish their chili, lock up, and drive home.

Jane put down her spoon and said, "That sounds like the Crosby train." Bower stood up, looked out the window over the lake, and saw a tornado barreling toward them. It was 6:08 p.m.

The next day, the Brainerd *Daily Dispatch* reported that the F3 tornado actually sounded like 40 freight trains and stretched half-a-mile wide.

Bower and Jane rushed from the main cabin and took shelter in the windward corner of the garage, the strongest building on the property. The tornado hit and the garage collapsed around them—a can of shellac spilled on Jane's head, and a cinderblock broke Bower's arm. As fate would have it, not so much as a window cracked in the main cabin—they could have eaten their chili unmolested as the twister roared past. The guest cabin took the brunt of the tornado, detonated into a million pieces. The tornado lifted the bunkhouse off its cinderblock foundation and set it down at the top of the hill.

The mile-long driveway blocked by felled trees, Bower went down to the lakeshore to find his boats and docks pushed up on shore by a tidal wave—residents at the other end of the lake claim that when the twister hit the water, they could see the lake bottom. Bower waved a red windbreaker over his head until someone at the Koonce place on the western shore saw him and came over in a fishing boat. Bower and Jane made their way to the hospital in Brainerd.

In a photo album dedicated to the tornado and its aftermath, yellowed newspaper clippings tell of the twister's destruction. Faded photographs under aging plastic show Bower, in a white t-shirt and khakis, surrounded by loggers with hard hats and chainsaws. There's my dad, skinny as I've ever seen him, sweeping out the skeleton of the half-destroyed garage. In a series of three photos, he confronts a snapping turtle that the tornado sucked up from the lake and deposited in the garage: he's looking down at the snapper; he thrusts a broom handle toward the prehistoric reptile; he carries the turtle away, hanging from the shaft by its prehensile jaws.

White pines, some of the oldest and largest in Minnesota, had escaped the loggers' saws for two centuries but now lay stacked like cordwood, eight to ten feet high in spots. Over the rest of that summer, Bower's beloved pines were hauled away, the guest cabin was rebuilt, and the bunkhouse was jacked up onto a Lincoln Log contraption of railroad ties and casters and rolled back on top of the reconstructed garage.

For years as a child, I'd look out over the swamp on the other side of the bluff and see the red bedspreads from the guest cabin hanging from the branches of dead tamaracks, like forgotten Christmas ornaments. Every summer the trees and the sheets sank a bit more into the swamp, until one summer I couldn't see them anymore. They'd been absorbed into the land.

When I was young, I didn't care much about the land. The forest was little more than an obstacle we drove through on our way to the lake. Snapshots show us as children, fishing for pumpkinseeds over the rails of the pontoon boat. If we rubbed against the side of the boat, the oxidized paint would smear a blue powder on our swimsuits; the red plywood decking was blisteringly hot on our bare feet. Bower wore a captain's hat when he piloted the pontoon; the adults got to sit on lawn chairs, the kids had to stand, and dogs were not allowed.

We caught leopard frogs for bass fishing, though I never once caught a fish on a live frog. When my brother and cousin got tired of fishing, they'd stick a lit firecracker in a frog's mouth, toss it into the lake, and laugh at the muted underwater explosion. With nightcrawlers on our hooks, we caught crappies and sunnies with nearly every cast. Mom would lay newspapers across the cedar dock and fillet the fish after we'd scraped away the scales. The heads and entrails were wrapped up in the newspaper and thrown over the bank toward the swamp, only to be discovered and consumed by the dogs. The one and only preparation of these panfish was breaded and fried in butter.

As kids, my brothers and I swam and skied and boated and suntanned and generally avoided the woods. I look back now and wonder how we could have ignored the acreage that has since become so important to me. Mosquitoes and deer flies and horseflies and poison ivy and thorns—that's what the forest held, we thought. Only in October, when all those had abated, would we hike through the woods, at least once in matching denim outfits for the family Christmas card photo.

Years later, the ownership of the land having passed from my grandparents to my parents' generation, I journeyed north with my wife and our young children. Our conflict came with us, like an unwanted cartop carrier full of venomous snakes. Several times in those years, we would arrive at the lake and unpack, and within minutes, after a fight, we'd be loading the gear and the kids back in the minivan to drive home. Sometimes I succeeded in brokering a temporary truce and salvaging the weekend, but other times we departed within an hour of our arrival. My cousin recently reminded me of a weekend during which she did not see my wife, only heard her through the baby monitor from the guest cabin.

When we moved back to Minnesota from New Jersey after our brief sojourn to the East Coast, we got permission to move up to the lake until the renters vacated our house in the suburbs. We lived in the guest cabin and fought. I struggle to remember much from the summer of 2004, but I distinctly recall a shouting match between my wife and my mother that concluded with my mother saying, "Well, I think you need to find a new place to live." And we did, though I cannot remember where.

After that, my wife asked me to promise her that we would never go to the family land again. And I did. I vowed to divorce myself from the land in order to avoid a divorce from her. Looking back now I can see how that was a false dilemma, how even making that bargain—and the myriad other bargains I made—could not save the blighted union. I was simply forestalling the inevitable.

Dorjee and Tsering are our neighbors these days. They moved to Minnesota from India, their parents having fled Tibet in the 1950s when China overran and absorbed their homeland. Neither Dorjee nor Tsering has been to Tibet. Recently Courtney and I were at their house to celebrate Losar, Tibetan New Year, and over a table weighed down with rice and stewed goat and pork ribs—they joked that they couldn't find any yak meat in Minnesota—Dorjee confessed that he wants to visit Tibet before he dies. He explained how difficult it is for a Tibetan to get a visa to travel there, and how Chinese authorities closely monitor anyone who visits. Nevertheless, he wants to go, to set his feet on the land that is his spiritual home. He pointed wistfully at a tapestry hanging on the dining room wall. "That is Potala Palace in Lhasa," he said. "That is where His Holiness Dalai Lama should live."

Tibet is just one of the sacred spots in the world that's under contention. As I write, we're only days removed from open conflict in Israel: Israeli settlers torched 30 Palestinian homes on the West Bank; Palestinians retaliated by killing two Israeli brothers; Israeli troops fired tear gas and bullets at Palestinians, injuring nearly 400. As you read these words, something similar has probably just happened.

In a story from the Gospels, Jesus was transfigured into a glowing presence with bleach-white garments, flanked by Moses and Elijah. Peter, wanting the moment to last, asked if he could build three tabernacles to memorialize the miracle. Jesus ignored him and walked down the mountain, eager to get back to preaching and healing—he had no time for building cathedrals. Today, of course, there's a monumental church on the Mount of Transfiguration.

Peter, the literary everyman of the Gospels, was simply voicing the natural human inclination: we like to return to spots where we have had significant spiritual experiences. Place matters to us. It's another paradox of religion, that traditions based on spiritual truths care so much about material places: Jerusalem, Mecca, Salt Lake City, the Vatican.

In the twelfth century, Giovanni di Pietro di Bernadone (nicknamed Francis) renounced his inheritance, shed his clothes in the piazza, and condemned the church's extravagance before fleeing his hometown of Assisi. He wandered the hills in a burlap-sack chasuble, vowing to preach to the wild animals if that's the only congregation he could muster, often staying at a small Benedictine oratory perched on the edge of a gorge on Monte Subasio.

A few years ago, Courtney and I hiked up the switchback road that climbs out of Assisi to the hermitage. Along our route, workers in blue jumpsuits climbed ladders and shook olives from trees into waiting nets. The sun shone, and we shed layers as we ascended. Staffed by a handful of Franciscans, we nodded *ciao* and proceeded past the modern buildings of the hermitage onto the gravel paths that lead into the woods. A simple monument marks the spot where Francis built a small shelter in a grotto and laid his head on a rock for a pillow. Fellow hermits followed him out there and lived in the woods—the first Franciscans.

Assisi is a spiritual place. I felt it when I first visited in 1989 and have on each subsequent visit. I've never been disappointed, and I'm not alone—pilgrims from around the world descend on Assisi every year, hoping to absorb some of Francis's magic.

However, I'm not one who believes that any square inch on this planet is ontologically superior to any other. We invest places with meaning, be it Jerusalem or Iona or Assisi or Mecca. These places are special and sacred because they've been trod by people we venerate. When I was waffling about a foreign study term in college, Professor Edward Bradley slapped his hand on the desk in his office in Reed Hall and nearly shouted, "Dammit, man, you must come to Rome with me—we'll walk in the footsteps of the saints!" I did go, and we did walk, and my life pivoted on an axis.

But the more mundane places—the places known only to me—have an even stronger spiritual hold on me. As I've aged, I've become more aware of how important our family land is to me—more important than the parquet platform in the church sanctuary, the spot where I was baptized, confirmed, married, and ordained, where I baptized my children and preached and rubbed ashes on foreheads. More significant than that is the spot where I field-dressed my first deer; the chairs on the deck overlooking the lake where Courtney put her feet in my lap as we were falling in love, as I was realizing that love was possible again; the path through the lily pads where I've thrown dummy after dummy to train three hunting dogs; the granite headstone under which rest the ashes of my father.

We're the most peripatetic people who've ever lived, traversing the continent and the globe for jobs and travel, often putting distance between us and the places that nurtured us when we were younger. This starves us, in a way.

Deep in these woods, my most sacred place, shotgun in hand, dogs circling me, I stand in the aspen and consider the tornado that knocked me flat.

Before, my life looked like an old-growth pine forest, the picturesque scene that comes as pre-loaded wallpaper on a computer; a stock photo, with imperfections airbrushed out. Everything was as it should have been, as it's expected to be.

But then a twister ripped through, uprooting the old growth, leaving my life a barren moonscape.

What has grown back isn't pretty, at least not in the conventional sense. Divorce, remarriage, ex-, stepparents, stepkids, foreclosure, attorneys, former pastor, fallen pastor, child support, spousal maintenance, credibly accused, parenting time, custody orders, restraining orders, cops, affidavits, hearings. These are the roots and stumps that trip me up, the thistles and shoots that grew up where the more majestic trees used to stand. It's a tangled mess, and I didn't walk through it without thorns drawing some blood. But now I can stand in the middle of this forest and recognize its beauty. My life is scrubby and thorny, but it's also verdurous, beautiful in its own way. New life shoots up, rooted in the tangled mess that lies beneath the dirt. Not always visible, but I know it's there. I feel it under my feet.

I walk on, whistling for the dogs. Eventually they come to heel, and I release them back to hunt. Not the ideal hunting dog for grouse, Labradors are neither stealthy nor pointy. But occasionally things work out. The dogs get birdy and rush into a thicket of hawthorn. A grouse flushes, gets airborne. I shoulder my gun and swing it. I take a shot. The grouse falls, tumbling through the branches.

That will be the only grouse I shoot this year. The old saw goes: You know what they call a grouse hunt? A walk in the woods with a gun. That's okay. I like walking in the woods with a gun. And these woods, these scrubby, thorny woods, they're growing, and that's beautiful.

I meet God here, God who is somehow responsible for, as far as we can tell, untold numbers of galaxies stretching across the cosmos toward the expanding edge of the universe, 46 billion light years away. But God is also curator of this little parcel of 276 acres in Nokay Lake Township, a tiny speck in the grand scheme of things, but supremely important to me.

I'll be buried here, not far from my father. My kids will walk these trails, I hope, and visit my grave. And, God willing, generations after them will, too.

I have been absorbed into this land.

4

Companions

Dogs are minor angels, and I don't mean that facetiously. They love
unconditionally, forgive immediately, are the truest of friends, willing
to do anything that makes us happy, etcetera. If we attributed some
of those qualities to a person we would say they are special. If they
had ALL of them, we would call them angelic.

—Jonathan Carroll, *Teaching the Dog to Read*

WE'D GOTTEN BEAUMONT IN THE WINTER OF 1997. HE CAME FROM A
farm in New Auburn, Minnesota. We sat in the farmhouse kitchen.
The farmer spoke with the accent of a Minnesotan who'd been raised
by German-émigré parents. He called his wife, *Mom*; as in, "Mom, go
get the dog's papers."

We wrapped our new yellow Labrador retriever puppy in t-shirts
we'd slept in for a week so he'd become familiar with our scents. He
dozed on her lap as I drove, and he represented the newly declared
commitment we'd made to one another: we were engaged, we'd bought
a house, and now we had a dog. Everything was breaking my way; God
was smiling on me.

Beaumont slept with those shirts for months in a crate next to our
bed. He grew quickly, as Labs do, and ate everything in sight, including
at least three pairs of underwear and a baseball, the winding of which
I had to extract from his anus by putting a plastic bag over my hand
and holding one end of the string while he awkwardly scooted away
from me.

I trained Beaumont a little. I wasn't a hunter yet, and therefore neither was he. I did not take him on my first hunts with Doug because those were pro-level hunts and Beaumont was not even an amateur. But I did hunt with him over the years—we learned it together, and he became a solid amateur. What he lacked as a hunting companion he more than made up for as a family pet: small kids in footie pajamas climbed all over him. During our Babylonian Captivity in New Jersey, we left Beaumont with a friend and returned to find him 20 pounds heavier and immeasurably sadder.

On August 29, 2008, the night that I finally moved out of the house, the lights from police cars lit up the night sky and flashed across the front of the house as I walked out for the last time. I'd served divorce papers that day, and on my lawyer's advice tried to stay in the house. The conflict, however, was too intense for that to work. So, I walked out before things got worse, and I took Beaumont. I considered him mine, perhaps unfairly, and thus I claimed him. I couldn't take the kids or even a duffel bag of clothes, but Beaumont dutifully followed me, slowly climbing into the back of the car. He was 12, the same age as our marriage. And like our marriage, I'd euthanize him before the year was out.

At first, Beaumont and I lived in my parents' basement. After about a week there, I was sitting in their kitchen talking to my mom. My dad walked in and said, "Don't trust that lawyer of yours. She's just out to make money off you. I know, I had lots of lawyers. All they want to do is bill you more hours."

I said that I didn't really know what else to do other than trust my lawyer. I wasn't really in any position to question her advice. I felt overwhelmed, drowning in conflict and debt.

My dad told me not to interrupt him.

I said I really didn't want to have this conversation right now.

He started yelling.

I yelled back.

I said I was going to leave, and I started walking for the door.

"Take your fucking dog, too!" he screamed after me.

I called for Beaumont and he followed me out another front door. He and I slept at a friend's house for a week. My mom slept elsewhere, too.

A few weeks later, Beaumont's breathing grew labored. He panted constantly, sometimes unable to sleep. And he drank enormous amounts of water, never sated.

I took him to the vet and she told me he had laryngeal paralysis, not uncommon in old Labs. The muscles of his larynx had weakened to the point that they couldn't keep his airway open, she explained, and the cartilage in his throat was collapsing. This gave him the feeling he wasn't getting enough air, causing him to pant, and the constant panting sent a message to his brain that he needed to drink more water. She told me she could perform a surgery that would probably clear up the issue. It would cost a few thousand dollars, she said.

Instead, I booked a field at a nearby shooting preserve and paid them to put four pheasants out among the cornstalks and milo. Crusty snow lay on the ground when Beaumont gingerly climbed out of the car. I loaded my shotgun and we moved out into the field. I knew we'd have to take it slow. I feared that if he pushed it too hard, he'd suffocate right there in front of me; but I also thought that wouldn't be a bad way for him to go.

Over the course of an hour, he flushed each of the four pheasants. I shot each, and he retrieved each. Having circled the field, we arrived back at the truck. I opened the tailgate, and Beaumont just stood there looking up at me, panting. I set down my shotgun and put my arms under him, just inside his front and back legs. His belly was wet with snow. I lifted him into the back of the truck. He collapsed, exhausted and struggling to breathe.

The next day, I drove back to the vet; she was unsympathetic. She told me I should get the surgery, that she knew Labs who lived to 14 or 15. I said no, today's the day. I'd made up my mind.

Beaumont lay on his side on the sterile exam room floor, fluorescent lights buzzing overhead. I sat down on the floor and cradled his head in my lap. The vet tech shaved a strip on his foreleg; the vet wrapped a band above the shaved area, found a vein, and slipped the needle in. Beaumont looked up at me, then closed his eyes and I listened as his breathing slowed and ceased. The vet and her assistant stepped out of the room to give me a moment. I got up and left before they returned, walking quickly past the counter and telling them I'd call tomorrow with the payment.

As I drove, volcanic emotion welled up within me. My eyes blurred with hot tears, my throat burned. I pulled over on the wrong side of the road next to a park and called my brother Andrew, weeping. He answered and I couldn't speak through the sobs. I cried uncontrollably for several minutes, the car idling and Andrew telling me through the car's speakerphone that it would be okay. He was going through a divorce, too. He cried on the other end of the line.

I picked up Beaumont's ashes a week later, and when the ground thawed in the spring I buried him at the family land, on a bluff overlooking the lake in which he'd swam for hours on end, and from which he'd even retrieved a couple ducks.

One theory posits that humans are human in large part because of dogs. It goes like this: eons ago, wolves started orbiting around the camps of proto-human tribes. As the wolves ventured closer, the proto-humans gave the wolves some food. The wolves ventured closer still, and the proto-humans gave them a little more food, like a boat circling around an anchor with an ever-shortening chain. Over time, the two species became acclimated to one another.

The canines stood guard over the proto-human camps all night, allowing the proto-humans to sleep, and as the proto-humans slept for hours at a time, unlike virtually any other animal, their brains grew bigger. Over tens of thousands of years, generations of humans developed larger and larger brains. And over those same tens of thousands of years, generations of wolves were welcomed into the proto-humans' camps and domesticated. By this theory, *Homo sapiens sapiens* exist because of our partnership with *Canis lupus familiaris*, and vice versa.

Some anthropologists suggest another layer of cooperation between the species. About 40,000 years ago, humans and Neanderthals were apex predators, battling for dominance on the European continent. Our ancestors and their new-found ally, the wolf-dog, teamed up to hunt: packs of dogs would hound large herbivores like bison, elk, and mammoths to exhaustion, then humans would close in with spears to finish the job, and the two species would share the meat. This Paleolithic alliance, which the Neanderthals lacked, allowed humans to become top dog in Europe. Canines then came with us across Beringia, and together populated North and South America.

I was dogless for over a year. I rented a house that was being prepped for sale. Like a divorcée cliché, I bought cheap IKEA bunk beds for the kids and a double bed for myself. Someone gave me an old TV, which sat on the floor in the corner of an otherwise barren living room. Another friend bought me a small couch, and I added three beanbags: pink, blue, and green, one for each kid. The good news was that I didn't have much to clean up before the county custody evaluators came to inspect my living conditions.

One day, the home's owner came and laid sticky plastic on all the pathways in the house. She asked if I wore shoes in the house. I said I didn't. She asked if the kids did. I said they didn't either. She looked at me skeptically.

The basement was a vast desert of white carpeting, with not one piece of furniture. I didn't go down there except when the kids were over, when we'd descend and have epic wrestling matches. The kids were 4, 7, and 8.

But mainly, I was alone. I did not have the kids often; Courtney and I were dating, but she lived in Dallas. And my friends from 20 years of ministry had fallen away like petals from a desiccated flower arrangement. I went to the gym twice a day. I went through a handle of gin and half a dozen limes per week. I sat in a beanbag chair and watched TV and googled "how dads get custody."

The time had come to list the house, the owner informed me. I had to move out. Needing to live in the kids' school district, I started looking for a place to rent. One had stained carpeting. Another had stained walls. Another had stained carpeting and walls. Then my parents stepped in. We'll buy a house, they said, and you can rent it from us. Once you get back on your feet, you can buy it from us. Humiliating, but I took the offer. They bought a house and I moved in.

Mike, a family friend in Menominee, Wisconsin, bred Labs, and I heard he had a yellow male from his last litter that had been returned to him. The dog was a year old, he said when I called. He'd give me the dog for $425. I didn't have $425. I must have mentioned this to Courtney because a week later a check for $425 arrived in the mail. She knew I needed a dog.

I drove the 90 minutes to Menominee. Mike introduced me to Albert, a fine-looking Lab with broad shoulders and a large, blocky head. Mike told me that he had shot a gun over Albert to make sure the dog wasn't gun-shy, but he hadn't done any training beyond that.

Doug came over to meet Albert, and he gave me a copy of James Lamb Free's 1949 classic, *Training Your Retriever*, rife with lines like: "Hold the dog firmly by the scruff of the neck with one hand, so he can't get away from you, and administer the licking with the other."[1]

Day after day, in the backyard I set up a baseball diamond arrangement with canvas dummies doused in duck scent. Training Albert gave me hope and purpose during the long stretches when I didn't see the kids, and my intense connection to him was cemented over the next couple years.

Albert's physique impressed, front shoulders of rippling muscle and a tight back end. But what was most noteworthy about Albert was his attack. Whether we were hunting a field for pheasants, the woods for grouse, or a slough for ducks, he dove in with complete and total commitment.

One time, hunting a cattail slough in South Dakota, I lost sight of Albert, but I heard him yelp—unusual since he was not a barker or growler. When I caught up with him, a two-inch flap of skin in the shape of a half-moon hung from his chest. He must have run into barbed wire at full speed. Back at the truck, I hoisted him onto the tailgate and my buddy Craig held him down while I used a surgical stapler that I carry in my dog first aid kit to attach the skin flap back to his chest. Albert did not so much as flinch as I sunk five staples into his flesh. We drove to the next field and I closed Albert in a crate when we marched off in search of more pheasants—he needed to heal, not hunt. Ten minutes later, he appeared by my side. He'd busted out of the kennel, an escaped prisoner, unwilling to forsake even one opportunity to chase birds.

The Great Chain of Being, requisite study material in my high school history class, was the medieval concept that everything in creation exists in a hierarchy. At the top is God, followed by angels, then the pope and the king, then priests and princes, then the rest of humankind. Below us are the animals, then plant life, then mineral matter. The beings at the top are incorporeal, pure spirit; the rocks at the bottom are pure matter, no spirit. Everything in between—including us—is a mix of spirit and matter. The theologians of the Middle Ages borrowed this concept from Aristotle, who'd ranked the animal kingdom: warm-blooded above cold-blooded; mammals above reptiles.

A thousand years after Aristotle, the church declared that the hierarchy was God-ordained and immutable. The feudal economy of medieval Europe was a reflection of the hierarchy, as was the polity of the Catholic Church. Only with the advent of the Enlightenment did the links in the chain start to weaken and snap, inspiring such phrases as "all men are created equal." But the Declaration of Independence doesn't claim that flora and fauna were endowed by their Creator with anything, much less individual rights. In fact, they're ignored altogether, not even mentioned in that anthropocentric document.

For some Christians, the conversation about our relationship with other animals begins and ends with Genesis 1:28, in which God tells Adam and Eve to be fruitful, multiply, fill the earth, and subdue it. That's the entirety of their theological justification for hunting and fishing: God told us to dominate the earth, so we hunt. Next question?

The Catholic Church is a bit more sophisticated about it, but still the magisterium pronounced as recently as the Second Vatican Council in 1965 that the human being is "the only creature on earth that God has willed for its own sake," implying that all other creatures were created for our sake. (To his credit, in 2015 Pope Francis walked that back a bit in *Laudato Si'*, warning against anthropocentrism and encouraging us to see ourselves in community with all living things.)

The Bible itself substantiates this view of the created order, even beyond that early verse from Genesis. The Hebrew and Christian scriptures don't offer a sophisticated animal ethic. Other religions have a bit more to say, but only a bit. Hinduism is ambivalent toward animals: on the one hand, Hindus who live less-than-stellar lives might be reincarnated as animals, a karmic punishment; on the other hand, monkeys and cows are venerated—even the milk of the cow is sacred: I once watched a penitent crawl up the 272 steps of the Batu Caves Temple in Malaysia with a brass bowl of cow's milk, kneeling on each step to pray. Buddhism teaches that we should strive for the end of all suffering, thus many Buddhists are vegetarians; but in their six realms of existence, the animal realm is evil. Islam joins the chorus: animals are provided by God for our use, "some for riding and some for your food," but mistreatment of animals is condemned.

In their origins, religions are anthropocentric. No surprise—they were developed to explain and regulate human interactions with God. Animals take a back seat; plants and dirt are an afterthought.

The intransigence of organized religions on this issue is one reason why they're struggling, because public sentiment about animals is changing, and quickly. In ancient Rome, staged hunts took place in the Colosseum and the Circus Maximus in which thousands of animals were slaughtered in front of tens of thousands of spectators; today, 70 percent of Americans are uncomfortable with animals performing in a circus. And while it might not have occurred to Thomas Jefferson, according to the Pew Survey, one-third of Americans today believe that animals should be afforded the same individual rights as humans. According to researchers who are tracking this trend, the more rights we've gotten as human persons, the more we want our fellow species to have the same.

And I hardly need to mention our relatively new concern for the bottom rungs on the medieval chain, plants and minerals. In the past, humans despoiled whole swaths of the planet without a second thought; now we're cleaning up our messes and trying to prevent new ones.

Care for the rest of creation, beyond our own species, is a mark of our cultural evolution. Few of us think of the created order as a hierarchical chain these days. A web is a more apt metaphor. We are woven into a fabric of creation that includes everything from the largest mammal to the smallest cell; everything in the fabric is interconnected to everything else.

This is the hunter's paradox. I sing a paean to one animal, my dog, my companion, while I'm out to kill another, my prey. Why does one sleep next to my bed and the other wind up on my grill? And why do I get to decide their respective fates?

Some would say that's the way God set it up: we're the masters of creation, and we get to determine which animal is food and which is a house pet. But that answer is shallow and unsatisfactory, a holdover of the old chain.

Admittedly, humans play an outsized role in the web of creation, and we do decide the fates of many species, through conservation, neglect, or extirpation. But if the evolutionary relationship between humans and canines shows us anything, it's that our survival is mutually beneficial. We've grown reliant upon one another. The dogs rely on us for survival, we feed and shelter them. Some species—hogs, camels—have jumped over and back across the half-court line that divides wildness and domesticity, but for dogs there's no going back.[2] Without humans, dogs won't make it—they've lost their killer instinct.

The math has recently changed on our side of the ledger, too: we no longer rely on dogs to help us put meat in the larder. The dog has gone from aiding our physical survival as guard and hunter to aiding our emotional and spiritual survival: thus millions of people testify that they couldn't make it through the day without their dogs. (Maybe *Homo sapiens sapiens* could exist without *Canis lupus familiaris*, but would we want to?)

In consideration of this paradox—I feed my dog, but I eat a squirrel—I'm drawn to consider the lesson of this unique interspecies partnership: it's taught me to lower my eyes.

The earliest images of Christians praying, painted on the walls of the Roman catacombs, show them in the "orant" position—standing, arms raised, palms up, eyes heavenward. God was up there, in the sky, at the top of the chain. To this day, pray-ers in worship settings assume the same posture, even though most of them probably believe in a spherical Earth, meaning that what's down for us is up for someone on the other side of the planet. There's really no such thing as "up" and "down," cosmically speaking. Nevertheless, that mental framework is tough to shake, so we keep looking up when we pray.

Hunting with dogs has cured me of that ailment. They've drawn my gaze downward, away from a vague hope for help from an immaterial being who lives in the sky and instead to a fellow creature with whom I'm collaborating on an activity that means more to each of us than anything else we do. Outside of my spouse and children, I am never more at-one with another being than when I'm hunting with my dog. As the poet and outdoorsman Jim Harrison wrote, "Quite literally you belong in the outdoors because your people spent five million years there, only recently emerging into nation- and city-states. The rituals of hunting and fishing, like those of gathering, are archetypally in your blood."[3] They're in my dog's blood, too. We share that in common. And when we're doing it together, the experience is transcendent, uniting me not just with his species, but with all species.

Untold extraordinary retrieves filled Albert's resumé. Once, hunting pheasants in South Dakota with Jorge and his buddy Greg, the latter hit a bird that flew into a neighboring field. We left our guns in the truck as darkness descended and walked the dogs into the snow-covered slough. After maybe 10 minutes of searching, the other guys were ready to give up. But I could tell that Albert was birdy, and I didn't want to pull him off the scent. If he was convinced that a bird was nearby, he simply would not quit until he found it. After a few more minutes, he stuck his snout under a clump of snow and grass. Then his entire head disappeared. And then he emerged with his jaws around a rooster.

Countless are the times that we were hunting in a long line of guys and their pointing dogs—a shot rang out and a bird fell, and after some minutes of fruitless searching I heard the plaintive cry over the prairie wind, "Hey, can you send your retriever over here?" Albert would not venture down the line without me, so together we'd hoof it through cover to help some hunter and his uninterested pointer find a missing pheasant. More often than not, Albert found the bird.

As invariably happens, Albert grew old. At the Best Western in Huron, after a long day of hunting he collapsed onto his bed. I gave him two pills, an anti-inflammatory and a pain killer. I filled a syringe with 1.25 ml of Adequan, the canine version of Glucosamine, tapped it to extract any air bubbles, and injected it into the thick skin on the back of his neck. The next morning his eyes were pussed shut from the lashes of a thousand cattails; I pressed a warm, wet washcloth over them and he moaned with relief. His front legs and chest bore scars from barbed wire, and he came back to me dripping bright red blood from his mouth more times than I care to remember, cut open by something deep in a blind thicket.

As Albert's life came to an end, I wondered if I would ever again have such a bond with a dog. He came to me at the lowest point in my life, and he walked alongside me through the valley of the shadow of death. I never saw him play with another dog, not once—he didn't care about them, only me. His commitment to me was absolute, the ancient homo sapiens-canine connection to the nth degree. When I walked through a field with Albert in search of game, he and I were mutually dependent. It was nothing less than a spiritual bond.

Having hunted with him for so many years, I could predict his movements, and he mine. Through whistles and staccato shouts, I made my wishes known to him. He in turn worked the apportioned territory, occasionally looking back at me to confirm that he was on the right path. In the early years, I could tell in a binary fashion whether or not he was on game: birdy or not birdy. Later, with hundreds of hours hunted together, I saw gradations of birdiness in his behavior, indicated by the vigor of his tail-wag, the angle of his ears, the zeal of his sniffing. His entire demeanor communicated to me how our hunt was going.

I relied on him to find and flush the quarry. He relied on me to down the bird with a blast. I relied on him for the retrieve. We were simpatico.

Courtney, the kids, and I got a puppy in 2018. Mike in Menominee didn't have a litter, but he gave me the name of a breeder in nearby Baldwin, Wisconsin. I drove out and met Jason, and he showed me a litter of Labs born a month earlier. I laid down a deposit and returned a month later with Aidan, who brought a pheasant wing tied to a string, which he dragged around the grass. One pup showed some interest in it, then another and another, but each had a short attention span for the pursuit. One yellow male, however, chased after that wing for a couple minutes. Aidan would let the puppy catch up to it, get his mouth around it, and get a snootful of the scent, then he'd tug it away. The puppy bounded after it, and the longer this game continued, the more we knew: this is the pup we want.

We named him Crosby. He's of slighter stature and lighter coat than Albert. For most of that fall, I heeded the advice of all the hunting handbooks that warn against taking a puppy afield. Then I remembered some wisdom that Grandpa Ralph, the Ford dealer, imparted to me. He'd retired by the time I bought my first car in the summer of 1990, between graduating from college and entering seminary. I drove my brand new Ford Probe to his house, and he stood with me on the driveway, admiring it. I told him how the dealer advised me not to drive over 60 miles-per-hour for the first thousand miles so the engine could break in over time.

He looked at me and said, "If it's ever gonna go 100, it's gonna go 100 today."

I jumped in the car, drove it out to a country road, and got it up over 100.

If Crosby was going to be a hunting dog, he might as well start straightaway. Those same hunting books urge you not to shoot over a puppy, lest you make the dog gun-shy. Instead, they counsel a staged approach, first clapping your hands, then clapping sticks together, then a starter's pistol, and finally a gunshot—breaking in the dog over a thousand miles.

I bothered with none of this, taking Crosby into the grouse woods when he was just shy of six months old. He showed no evidence that he understood his job, but he did follow Albert back and forth. A grouse flushed and flew straight over my head. I emptied both barrels of my over-under and missed twice. I immediately looked for Crosby to see if he'd been traumatized by the blasts. He was unconcerned, chasing after his mentor.

I didn't dare take Crosby with me to South Dakota early in the season of his first year—too much pressure not to screw up the hunt for other guys and their dogs. But late in the season, with a smaller hunting party and a couple more months of life under his collar—and with Albert sick at home—Crosby accompanied me as I drove west.

Over the course of four days, I watched him improve, each day building on the day before. On day one, he stuck close to my boots, and I had to encourage him to move out in front of me. I didn't care much if his nose was up or down, I just wanted him to get the rhythm of working a field.

On the second day, he started to range out in front of me without much encouragement. Occasionally he'd bump a bird, probably by accident, which startled him, but I overwhelmed him with praise so he'd know that's exactly what he's supposed to do.

On day three, he and I were blocking at the east end of a shelter-belt, positioned on a gravel road. Crosby was doing a nice job of sitting at heel when a rooster cackled and flushed out of the sorghum in front of us. I fired and the bird dropped dead right in the middle of the road about 20 yards away. I sent Crosby to go get that pheasant. He ran over to it, stood over it, and sniffed it. "Fetch it up!" I yelled, clapping my hands and coaxing him to bring that bird to me like he'd brought tennis balls and canvas dummies many times. He put his mouth over the pheasant, then pulled back. I shouted encouragement and he tried again. Finally he got a hold of the bird's wing and half-dragged, half-carried the rooster to me.

That experience sparked something in him, and by day four he needed neither encouragement nor direction. His instincts had been rewarded, and now he relied on them.

The next fall the three of us hunted together—Albert the wise veteran, Crosby nipping at his heels. We visited all of our favorite South Dakota fields, and we drove 1,800 miles to Oregon to duck hunt with my brothers. After one of those hunts, Albert could not stop shaking. We wrapped him in blankets and stoked the fire in the cabin's stove, but the convulsions went on for hours.

Back home, Albert struggled to eat. He'd swallow some food, cough, gasp for breath, and then eat some more. We took him to the vet, and an X-ray showed cloudy lungs and swollen lymph glands constricting his airway. After ruling out other possible afflictions, our vet gave us the diagnosis: lymphoma.

She started him on a steroid to shrink his swollen glands, which provided immediate relief. Nevertheless his prognosis was dire.

Just as I had with Beaumont, I drove Albert to a hunting preserve, and I asked them to put four pheasants in a field. I opened the door of the truck and Albert climbed down. For the next 45 minutes, he hunted hard, nose to the ground, quartering in front of me. Almost like he didn't have cancer.

One by one, he flushed the roosters, I shot them, and he retrieved them. He climbed back into the truck, exhausted, and slept the whole way home.

We loved Albert in the last days, inviting him onto the bed, giving him extra treats. But a week after that final hunt, he stopped eating and his breathing was disconcertingly rapid. We laid a dog bed in the backyard, and a vet from an at-home euthanasia service met us there. In a small consolation of the pandemic, my college kids were home, so we could all gather around Albert as he took his final breaths. He's buried next to Beaumont, overlooking the lake.

One dog is not a replacement for the other. They each occupy a unique place in my life. Beaumont lived and died with my first marriage. Albert accompanied me as I rebuilt my devastated life. And now Crosby journeys with me into the new wild places. These three dogs don't just mark the three chapters of my adult life. They have also reoriented my theology—my perspective on the whole created order, and whether there even is an "order." It's more of a woven web in which some threads are thicker than others—the strand between dog and human is among the thickest. But whether closely linked or distantly related, all are connected.

5

Predator

To match a Runao, stride by stride, heartbeat by heartbeat, was to transcend the self, to lose all consciousness of separation until you were one with the prey. And then: to reach out from behind, to grip a doe's ankle and bring her down into a headlock, to lift the jaw and expose the throat, slicing through it with a single clean action—to do all this and to eat the meat in the end—was to survive your own death: to die with the prey and yet to live again.

—Mary Doria Russell, *Children of God*

I'M STANDING AT THE CORNER OF A TWO-ACRE SQUARE OF SWITCHGRASS that sits in the middle of a harvested cornfield. Earlier today, a giant combine sucked up stalks, stripped them of ears, and spewed out silage in its wake. The pheasants that had been feeding in the corn, we figure, have fled into the relative safety of the switchgrass, around the perimeter of which stand: Larry, who, like me, had to rebuild his life after a failed marriage; his son, Jeremy, who will be shot by another hunter in a month; Jorge, who has throat cancer; Jorge's son, Nick, who doesn't have his kids this weekend; and my son, Aidan, who's in eighth grade and was suspended from school last week for getting in a fight—he's been struggling ever since his mom moved a thousand miles away last February.

These are my fellow wounded predators.

We're pinching. As opposed to our usual method of pushing-and-posting the big fields, we have surrounded this small piece. At Jorge's command, we release the dogs into the grass, then we follow. I walk an irregular pattern, a crooked path, stopping, starting again, stomping my feet—if I walk in a straight line, pheasants will wait me out, and when

I've passed, they'll escape. I'm trying to discombobulate them, to stalk them as other predators do.

A bird flushes. Someone yells, "Rooster!" I hear a shot and see a bird tumble from the sky. It lands near Aidan, tendrils of gun smoke winding out of his barrel. I let out a yawp.

I'm not usually one to celebrate a kill. I might say, "Nice shot," but I avoid the high-fives and back-slaps common on hunting TV shows. I don't call hunting or fishing a "sport," and I'm not after trophies or wall mounts. My whoop for Aidan is an exception to the rule—expressing joy for him, not celebrating the dead bird at his feet. Predators should not celebrate the death of the prey.

I once asked Jorge: what's the magic of hunting? "It's the combination of skill and cosmic forces," he said, avoiding the word *luck*. "The hunter must bring expertise and experience to the hunt, but also the stars need to align." In other words, I could be the greatest duck hunter in the world, but if the ducks aren't flying on the day I put out my decoys and lay in wait in the bullrushes, I won't shoot any ducks.

We didn't know if there would be any pheasants in this square of switchgrass. But in we walked, full of hope. One got up. Aidan shot it. And he deserves some cosmic kismet.

I've tried to figure out this passion for the outdoors that's come in the seventh inning of my life. My initial answer was the concentration required: "Most of our hunting days are relatively wordless, a testament to the quality of attention the sport requires, the absolute absorption in the day itself."[1] In a world of beeps and vibrations and red-dot notifications, my activities in the outdoors—hunting specifically—demand total, unmitigated focus. Walking through a field with other hunters, each of whom has a loaded firearm; trying not to break an ankle on a portage slick with mud and shards of granite with a 70-pound canoe on my shoulders; tracking an elk up a mountainside of shifting scree; sitting perfectly still for minutes on end as a tom turkey slowly pecks his way across a tilled field—these are not endeavors to be entered into unadvisedly or lightly, but reverently, deliberately, and with the utmost concentration. My outdoors activities demand from me a single-minded focus unlike anything else in my life. The older I get and the more that technology encroaches, the more I want something that demands so much of me.

When I've lost that concentration, bad things have happened. Last year I missed a deer because when I heard him behind me, I spun around and looked him in the eye. He bolted before I could raise my rifle. And a few years before that, while pheasant hunting, Jorge and Craig and their dogs pushed a quarter-mile-long tree belt toward me; I was posted at the far end, the beneficiary of their long walk through thorny Russian olive trees. Two roosters, one after the other, flew out of the trees, offering me easy shots, lay-ups. I missed them both. I'd been distracted, thinking about how things weren't going well at work, mentally spinning in a downward spiral of dejection and anxiety. I'd lost focus.

I confessed my sin and Craig absolved me. Jorge nodded in agreement. Six months earlier, I'd visited Jorge at the Mayo Clinic. When I walked up to the building that houses out-of-town cancer patients, I saw him standing against a brick wall, warming himself in the sun, but I didn't recognize him. His face gaunt and lopsided from oncologists slicing away at his throat, he couldn't have weighed more than 130 pounds. A week later, he collapsed in an elevator in that building, hit his head on the way down, and needed CPR to keep him alive.

Maybe your problems aren't so bad, says the man with throat cancer—without having to say it.

The cosmic forces had smiled on me, and in return I ignored them. I neglected my half of Jorge's equation for a successful hunt, the part about the hunter bringing all of his skill to the endeavor.

While the focus required remains an important aspect of why I spend time in wild places, I've discovered a deeper, more primal reason, to which I was awakened by two women hunters.

Jill Carroll's "Predation & The Way of All Things," is hidden like a hare in a thicket, a two-page essay in the middle of an academic monograph, and it's the best thing I've ever read on hunting.

"I hunt to eat," she begins.

Specifically, I hunt because I'm a carnivore, and eating meat from animals I myself have killed is the most ethical way I have found to be a carnivore. I don't know if that makes me human—more than I would be otherwise, or more than people who don't hunt. What I do know, most certainly, is that to hunt reminds me of my humanity, more than any other activity in which I participate.[2]

Carroll, a scholar of world religions, is an avid hunter, angler, and gardener, and has been since childhood. "As I see it, predation is hardwired into existence," she writes. Even in her garden, herbivores and parasites deal death, then their own corpses in turn become humus, composted into food that's consumed by plants. We'll each be eaten in the end, she reminds us, because "it's part of the contract of life on this marble planet."

I love her conclusion so much that I will quote it in full:

> When I take to the field with my shotgun to hunt, I say "Yes" to the world as it is, and to my place within it. I am a human animal alongside all the other animals, living and dying, eating and being eaten. I accept this reality; I accept my place within this reality. I am not willing to estrange myself from the world by morally condemning this fundamental aspect of our larger existence. To morally condemn predation would be to condemn the whole world. I can't bring myself to do that. I love the world too much.[3]

Carroll is honest about her place in the cycle of predation, unflinching in her acknowledgment that she's both a predator and, ultimately, prey, which is true for each of us, in spite of the fact that we've developed an entire economy around trying to avoid this truth—our meat is slaughtered and butchered where we never see it or smell it, and our own illnesses and death are hidden away in the sanitized sanctuaries of hospitals and funeral homes. Unlike our ancestors, we can go about our day-to-day lives without confronting the truth that we are predators, and we are preyed upon.

Yet the story of life on this planet is this very cycle. Every species' survival over time relies on the pattern: procreate before falling prey to death; consume others before being consumed. We should see this as a spiritual rhythm. Our ancestors did. Festivals of harvest and sacrifices of the most prized and fatted livestock marked time; funerals were rites during which the body of the deceased was wept over, seen, and touched. They understood themselves to be part of the cycle of predation.

"The central paradox of hunting is the painful paradox of life itself: Some of us live because others die," writes Mary Zeiss Stange in *Woman the Hunter*. We've tried to hide this reality by manufacturing "dualities (human/animal, warm-blooded/cold-blooded, animal/plant) that facilitate the construction of hierarchies of consumption." But those dualities collapse and the hierarchies fall like a house of cards the moment that a consumer becomes the consumed: "The deer's blood is as red and as warm as the hunter's own; her eyes, so lately luminous, as brown. Those who receive their food second- and third-hand can, if they choose, look away from this fact. A hunter cannot."[4]

Carroll and Stange call us to something—call us *back* to an acknowledgment that we do not stand at a remove from everything else in creation, somehow exempt from the rhythms of life-and-death, predator-and-preyed-upon. In truth, we swim in the same ocean as every other species on the planet, and there's blood in the water.

However, one of the issues for us, as the most rational actors in this drama of predator and prey, is that not all species are the same. There's a reason that the Great Chain of Being was so influential for so long, because we can see and categorize the differences between us and other creatures. As a child, I thought nothing of hooking a fish: pulling it from the water as blood dripped from its gills, watching it thrash on the bottom of the boat, cutting off its head. To go from fishing to hunting birds wasn't much of a leap, because they're also difficult to anthropomorphize. They don't look or act anything like us—they swim, they fly, they're covered with scales or feathers, they're cold-blooded, they lay eggs.

Deer are another story. I waited a long time before I killed my first deer. Stange is right: deer have luminous brown eyes. And they have beautiful, long eyelashes, like us. Let's call it the Eyelash Rule: the more an animal looks and acts like us, the less comfortable we are with killing it. Every time someone says to me, "I could never kill a deer," I ask, "Do you fish?" Usually they do, or they have in the past, or they have no problem with it. But they've drawn an invisible line somewhere between the small, scaly, cold-blooded aquatic creatures and the large, furry, warm-blooded mammals; they'll prey on animals on one side of that line but not the other.

Carroll and Stange put the lie to that line, because it's nearly impossible to establish objective criteria for which animals can be eaten and which cannot. Your ethical standard will inevitably be personal and subjective, and different from mine. The first time this dawned on me was as a college student, living in Rome. A few of us had pitched in on a hot plate and pot so that we could cook cheap lunches in our room and save our money for dinners out at nice restaurants. I bought a pack of hot dogs and dropped a couple in the pot. As they bounced in the boiling water, I practiced my Italian by reading the list of ingredients on the package, which included "*carne di cavalo*"—horse meat. I ate the wieners, but my classmates refused.

Horse is one thing, varmint is another. I once got a gig speaking at a junior high lock-in, which is when a group of kids stays up all night in a church. I delivered my sermon to the sleepy teens at 2 a.m.; as I spoke, an odor emanated from the church kitchen into the fellowship hall. I said my closing prayer, and two 18-year-old guys in Carhartt coveralls emerged from the church kitchen with three roasted animals on a sheet pan and asked, "Who wants to try raccoon, possum, and skunk?" I did. They weren't good. In fact, they were disgusting.

The "disgust mechanism" is a valuable evolutionary trait, protecting us from the pathogens in stuff like vomit and rotting meat. The next time you see a dog eating its own feces, you can say a prayer of thanks for your disgust mechanism. But it can go too far. Arachnophobia is an irrational extension of the disgust mechanism, as is fear of needles, obsessive-compulsive disorders that involve excessive cleaning, and many other psychopathologies. It's why most of us don't eat insects, even though they're a clean, cheap protein.

Then there's the other side of the coin of disgust: anthropomorphism. That's our tendency to attribute human behaviors and emotions to animals. When someone justifies their angling by saying that fish don't feel pain, but they would never kill an animal that suffers, like a deer, they're saying that the deer is like us and the fish is not, even though they really have no way of knowing the subjective experience of pain in a fish or a deer. Others discriminate on the basis of sentience, eating non-sentient beings but not sentient ones. Sentience, however, is notoriously difficult to determine (just ask your friendly neighborhood artificial intelligence bot).

In a stroke of cosmic genius, dogs evolved over time to have a muscle between their eyes that wolves lack, a muscle that makes their eyes look "cute" or "sad." The levator anguli oculi medialis muscle gave some wolves a leg up about 33,000 years ago because with the ability to raise their inner eyebrows, they bonded with humans and therefore got more food.[5] Eyelashes on deer serve the same function, protecting them from humans who won't hunt an animal with eyelashes. Needless to say, a hungry wolf doesn't notice a deer's eyelashes—both the disgust mechanism and anthropomorphism seem to be exclusively human.

Differences between species are real.[6] But you'd be hard-pressed to develop an objective ethical system that differentiates between animals with scales and animals with fur, or favors one species because of an extra eyebrow muscle. Ancient Hebrews judged some animals by their feet, eating the unclovened-hooved but not the cloven-hooved, a dietary guideline that made perfect sense for millennia but most of us today reject as arbitrary.

So instead, let's start the process of determining which animals are our prey and which are not with Carroll's admonition: we're in this world, fully human, and fully a part of the cycle of predation. From within it, not over above it, we begin.

I'm not going to eat my dog. I have a different relationship with him than I do with an elk. Crosby is my companion and my hunting partner, he brings me spiritual sustenance, and I value him for that. The elk that I hunt will bring me sustenance as well, more physical than spiritual.

Even famous hunters have their limits. Jim Harrison "wouldn't shoot a bear for a million dollars." He'd lived with bears in the Upper Peninsula of Michigan for decades and had "developed a pleasantly complicated relationship with them to the degree that I couldn't eat bear meat without bear nightmares."[7]

And in a well-known section of *A Sand County Almanac*, Aldo Leopold tells of how, as a young man, he and some buddies saw a mother wolf with her pups. "In those days we had never heard of passing up a chance to kill a wolf. In a second we were pumping lead into the pack." They mortally wounded the adult and crippled a pup: "We reached the old wolf in time to watch a fierce green fire dying in her eyes. I realized then, and have known ever since, that there was something new to me in those eyes—something known only to her and the mountain."

At the time, Leopold thought that fewer wolves meant more deer for him and his buddies to hunt. But what he learned in the decades that followed is what the she-wolf and the mountain had known for millennia: predators and prey live in a symbiotic relationship. If the wolves disappear, the deer will destroy the mountain. And by the time he wrote these words, many years after he shot the wolf, he'd seen just that:

> I have seen every edible tree defoliated to the height of a saddle-horn. Such a mountain looks as if someone had given God a pruning shears, and forbidden Him all other exercise. . . . I now suspect that just as a deer herd lives in mortal fear of its wolves, so does a mountain live in mortal fear of its deer. And perhaps with better cause, for while a buck pulled down by wolves can be replaced in two or three years a range pulled down by too many deer may fail of replacement in as many decades.[8]

Both Harrison and Leopold drew lines between what animals they would hunt and what they would not, and they came by the opinions honestly, after many years of stomping around wild places. Each was a hunter and predator, but each was also a renowned conservationist. Their time in wild places, not grocery stores, made them more deliberate predators.

Hunting has always been about survival. I imagine aboriginal hunters, stalking the same land that I do, in search of buffalo, deer, hare, and fowl. Hunting was their subsistence. They hunted to survive.

I also hunt to survive. Mine is an emotional survival. A spiritual survival.

Trauma hit me in two surges: the divorce itself, then the aftermath. The first, like a bigger-than-expected wave, caught me standing knee-deep in surf and knocked me sideways; then, as I was regaining my balance, the second wave hit, threw me to the seafloor, and washing-machined me senseless.

I had a recurring dream during those years that I was screaming for rescue at the top of my lungs, but no sound came from my mouth. The harder I screamed, the more panic I felt, but still no sound. No one could hear me.

Panic is one word that describes my experience for the better part of a decade. Anguish is another. So is terror. Those three unwanted guests invaded every aspect of my life, waking me in the middle of the night and stalking me during the day. The earth didn't spin a revolution without one or more of them afflicting me. They were my predators. I'd been a person of deliberate faith and religion since youth— those are related but distinct. Religion is the skeleton, providing the structure, and faith is the flesh-and-blood that brings the creature to life. But like a man flayed, panic, anguish, and terror peeled the flesh from my bones. Without the faith, the religion didn't hold together.

As I regained my footing, I took stock of my life. I looked around and evaluated what I had and who I was. I had custody of my kids; I was in love; I had parents and brothers and cousins; and while a lot of my ministry colleagues abandoned me, my hunting buddies stuck with me.

When I visited wild places, the despair wasn't so bad. Hunting and fishing and hiking and canoeing got my mind off my problems and reminded me of my connection with—my reliance on—the rest of creation. Wild places put everything in perspective, and wild places demanded my concentration.

When insomnia hit, I used to pray an old Orthodox prayer: "Lord Jesus Christ, Son of God, have mercy on me, a sinner." I prayed those words in coordination with my breath, my fingers working the hundred knots of a prayer rope made by monks, and that usually eased me back to sleep. The rope now hangs abandoned on a drawer knob below a shelf that holds the detritus of my religious life: icons, hymnbooks, crosses. Now when I can't sleep, I close my eyes and travel to a wild place. It might be sitting in a deer stand in the November woods, listening for the crunch of hooves on brittle, frosty leaves; or pulling a canoe paddle silently through water, leaving a swirl in its wake; or sitting in a duck blind with my brothers, watching snow fall silently, absorbed into a pond.

My outdoors meditations calm me as much as traditional prayer ever did, delivering me the peace I crave by putting me in touch with the sublime. When panic, anguish, and terror come to call in the wee hours, I go to the woods, where I'm thrust into the delightful horror built into the creation, the cycle of predation from which no creature is exempt. This is my prayer, to the God of wild places.

I had expected to be religious until I died. I had mastered religion, its language and liturgies, its rhythms and rites. I had become both a master and a doctor of religion.

But now being outdoors consumes my imagination, and I'm learning the language and patterns of the woods.

We walk around every day like we're the apex predator, top of the food chain, nothing to fear. In a way, of course, that's right, and that's why there are 7.5 billion of us and counting. But the truth is, predators *are* stalking me. Not saber-tooth tigers or short-faced bears, both of which hunted my ancestors, but cancer, heart disease, Alzheimer's, Parkinson's. Those are my predators. And one of them will eventually get me.

I live in the cycle of predation. When I slap a mosquito, accidentally step on an ant, or drive over a squirrel dashing across a suburban street, I'm a predator, as I am when I till my garden or shoot an elk or order a hamburger.

Cancer is Jorge's predator.

When a pheasant rooster flushes wild 10 feet in front of a charging dog, he is fleeing a predator. Maybe I, working in tandem with my canine partner, can shoulder my 12-gauge fast enough and shoot true enough to drop that bird. Or maybe he escapes, flying a half-mile and landing safely in another field. And maybe there's a coyote waiting in that field, hoping for an unsuspecting pheasant to strut her way.

And maybe the surgery to remove the tumor in Jorge's throat, the chemotherapy and proton radiation at the Mayo Clinic, the prayer and meditation, maybe these will allow Jorge to rebuff his predator. Or maybe not.

Even if the cancer doesn't get him, something will, just as something will get me.

As a wise king said 2,500 years ago, "To every thing there is a season, and a time to every purpose under the heaven: a time to be born, and a time to die; a time to plant, and a time to pluck up that which is planted; a time to kill, and a time to heal." He could have added: a time to be predator, and a time to be prey.

I am predator, and I am prey. But that's not something that religion ever prepared me for. I cannot recall a single sermon or seminary lecture about my place in that cycle. Instead I sat in a pew for years, thinking only of myself, my needs and wants and desires and fears. How would God tend to *me* or to *my* loved ones? We'd pray and pray for God to do something miraculous, to intervene in someone's body and magically excise cancer. Never did we acknowledge cancer as our predator, or ourselves as predators of the roasted chicken we'd eat in the fellowship hall after the service.

It wasn't always so. Ancient people acknowledged the relationship between themselves and the animals on which they preyed, and that relationship was honored in myths and rituals. "The basic hunting myth is a kind of covenant between the animal world and the human world," said master mythologist Joseph Campbell. "The animal gives its life willingly, with the understanding that its life transcends its physical entity and will be returned to the soil . . . through some ritual of restoration."[9]

Not long ago, I had conversations with two very different hunters: an elderly Catholic priest of the Passionist Order, and a young trans-masculine, pagan huntress. Each told me a story about hunting deer, and each said virtually the same thing: when they shot the deer, they had the sense that the deer was giving itself to them, that the deer had some kind of agency in the encounter. In spite of their dramatically different religious commitments, each of these hunters was tapping into an ancient ethos in which the prey animal and the human predator have a conscious exchange based on mutual respect.

Ancient people did not take the kill for granted, as we too often do today. For the Native Americans who inhabited the Plains, the buffalo hunt was infused with religious ritual, as was the salmon run for the indigenous people of the Pacific Northwest and the eland hunt for the Bushmen of the East African savannah. The first bite of raw meat was a eucharist of sorts, and the valor and ferocity of the animal lived on in tales told of the hunt around campfires for years.

Campbell says that the myths that grew up around the hunt were meant to assuage the guilt for the kill, turning the animal into an emissary from God, carrying a divine message: "The religious attitude toward the principal animal is one of reverence and respect, and not only that—submission to the inspiration of that animal. The animal is the one that brings gifts."[10]

In the early church, the story was told of St. Eustachius.[11] In the time of Augustus Trajan, there was a soldier named Placidus. He was a fine soldier. One day, on leave from the army, he went with some other men into the woods to hunt. Placidus found the trail of a deer and followed it deeper into the woods, away from the rest of the hunting party. He came to a clearing, and there he saw a massive, beautiful stag. He nocked an arrow and drew back his bowstring.

Then the stag turned toward him. Placidus saw something between the stag's antlers, something glowing, shining like the sun in miniature, taking the form of a cross. It was the cross of Christ. The beast spoke, saying, "Return to Rome and be baptized in the name of the Father, Son, and Holy Spirit. Have your wife and sons baptized as well. And hunt no more. From this day forward, you shall be called Eustachius, which means *steadfast*."

The stag began showing up in his dreams, warning him of great calamities that were to befall his family. And just as the animal prophesied, Eustachius and his family lost everything and were sent on the run as refugees, far from Rome.

They arrived at a rushing river but could not even afford to hire the bargeman to take them over. So Eustachius carried his sons across, one at a time. He dropped the first son on the far side of the river, and as he was going back to get the second son, the first son was grabbed in the jaws of a lion and taken away. He then dropped the second son on the far side of the river, and as he was going back to get his wife, the second son was snatched by a wolf. As Eustachius swam back across the river, trying in vain to save his sons, the barge pilot stole his wife and floated away down the river with her.

Utterly alone and without any belongings or money, Eustachius spent the next 15 years guarding farmers' flocks, sleeping in their fields at night, and praying to the Lord. One day, two messengers of Augustus Trajan approached him and said that the emperor needed him back in Rome to quell a revolt, since he was one of the greatest warriors alive. He did as the emperor asked, and Trajan then made him a general and sent him to the frontier where he won many battles.

During one such battle, his troops overran a village and, after killing a captain in the opposing army, that captain's wife recognized Eustachius as her true husband and ran into his arms. Meanwhile, two captured soldiers were brought to him, claiming they had been raised by wild animals, and Eustachius recognized the young men as his sons. Eustachius and his family returned to Rome and were invited to the Palatine palace for a dinner to celebrate his many victories. But the new emperor, Augustus Hadrian, was no friend to Christians. When he discovered that the family dining at his table were Christians, he ordered them to make an offering to the gods of Rome. They refused, steadfast in their faith in the Lord.

Hadrian had the family jailed that night, and the next morning they were thrown into a pit of hungry lions. But the lions did not touch them, for the son who was raised by a lion knew how to speak with lions. The next day they were thrown into a den of hungry wolves, but the son who was raised by a wolf told the wolves not to eat them.

Finally, on the third day, Hadrian had the family thrown into a furnace. Although they died, their bodies were not consumed, and the Christians of Rome retrieved them and placed them in the catacombs, where they were venerated for years.

Eustachius's revelation was later conflated with St. Hubert, an eighth century Belgian nobleman who was crazy about hunting. He, too, encountered a stag sporting a crucifix between his antlers, and he, too, converted. Later hagiographies record a sermon the stag gave the hunter, expounding on the ethics of the hunt. The hunter should have compassion for the prey, preached the deer, should always take clean shots, should not shoot a trophy buck when an injured deer is available, and should not kill a doe who has a fawn in tow.

In this medieval tale, the predator and the prey are in conversation about their relationship. The first ethical code of hunting was not written by a hunter but by the hunted. The stag represents the hunter's conscience, the voice of every animal the hunter has killed and will kill.

Eustachius died in 118. His feast day is September 20, right at the start of hunting season.

Hubert died in 727 after a long and fruitful career as a bishop. His feast day is November 3, right when I hunt deer each year. He is the patron saint of hunters.

6

Failure

For those who would seek directly, by entering the primary temple, the wilderness can be a ferocious teacher, rapidly stripping down the inexperienced or careless. It is easy to make the mistakes that will bring one to extremity.

—Gary Snyder, *The Practice of the Wild*

THE LEADEN SKY HANGS LOW AS I EXIT MY TRUCK WITH A SHOTGUN, a mug of coffee, and three turkey decoys. I walk up the Tornado Road on our family land to the point where it turns from south to east, coming to a small clearing that encircles a bur oak tree. I know that wild turkeys frequent this spot because I've caught images of them on a trail camera. After roosting in tall trees, they fly down into the forest, group up, and warily make their way toward the Johnsons' field, where they root for grubs and seeds. I have photographic evidence that the small clearing where I put out my decoys is often trafficked by turkeys.

Last year I set up not far from here, in the power line cut. After waiting and calling for several hours, I heard something behind me, and ever-so-slowly I turned my head. I caught a glimpse of a beard hanging from the chest of a turkey—a male. Perfect, I thought. He's going to come around and make a beeline for the hen decoy that I'd staked in the ground 20 yards in front of me. Except he didn't. He vanished.

The year before that I was sitting down along the swamp when I looked up toward the road and saw the head of a turkey bobbing up and down just above the berm. I aimed my gun but never had a clear shot.

The year prior to that, again in the power line cut, I called back and forth with several toms and jakes for an hour after sunrise. When they finally left their roosts, they soared far overhead, landed at the edge of the cornfield, and sprinted out of range.

And every year for the past decade, the same: I hunt wild turkeys, without success.

At age 12, the ink not yet dry on his first turkey license, Aidan shot one—probably more of that cosmic karma that keeps flowing his way. But still, even my prepubescent son had successfully bagged a turkey. I recommitted myself. This would be the year. I'd scouted and prepared, and I was ready to wait as long as I had to.

On the first morning, I saw nothing and heard nothing. Same on the second, but I remained resolute.

Now day three in the same spot, doubts creep in. Maybe since the trail cam photos, the turkeys have altered their pattern. Maybe I spooked them.

But then, on the far side of the cornfield, I see a pair slowly bobbing their way toward me. I raise my binoculars and confirm that they're not geese or sandhill cranes, they're turkeys. Today is my day. I can feel it.

Over the course of the next hour, the birds slowly work their way across the field. They jab at the soil with their beaks, then stop, lift their heads, look around warily, and return to pecking.

For the most part, I lay off my call, worried that my zeal will alarm them. When they've halved the distance between us, my heart sinks. They're hens, not jakes. I can't shoot them. But I console myself that they might attract a rutting male. I wait for another hour.

At about 50 yards, they casually saunter into the woods. No tom or jake ever appears. All denouement, no climax.

In spite of his early success turkey hunting, Aidan is not unacquainted with failure. On his first trip to South Dakota, we surrounded the same square of switchgrass where he'd have success two years later. Jorge generously positioned Aidan on the corner of the field where he suspected the birds would funnel out, and he wasn't wrong. When the dogs ran into the grass, pheasants boiled up, many of them flying right at Aidan. He shot three times, reloaded, shot three more times, and missed all six pheasants. We climbed into Jorge's truck—Jorge and me in front, Jorge's son, Nick, and Aidan in back. Tears of frustration and embarrassment squeezed out of Aidan's eyes, his anger filling the cab. Before I could say anything by way of comfort or admonition, Nick spoke up with wisdom beyond his 30 years: "Missing is part of hunting. I've shot thousands of shells through this gun, and I've missed more times than I've hit. So don't beat yourself up. We all miss. A lot."

Aidan let out a sigh. I didn't turn around, and I somehow found the self-discipline not to elaborate on Nick's homily. We rode on in silence. I considered the lesson for myself: I'd hung on to a marriage that nearly killed me because I thought I could make it work—really, because I didn't want to confront the truth that I'd failed at it. I didn't want that failure hanging around my neck the rest of my life.

My religion didn't adequately prepare me for failure. Take, for example, prayer, arguably the practice most central to Christianity. "Prayer works," reads the bumper sticker in defiance of our real-world experience. I've spent a lot of time in church small groups and Bible studies considering why God did not answer certain prayers: maybe we didn't pray hard enough, or didn't use the right words; maybe it wasn't God's will. But we never considered the possibility that prayer just doesn't work some of the time. (A lot of the time.) Instead, unanswered prayers are explained away: God doesn't fail to answer prayers, God just answers them differently than you'd hoped. Answers like that come from a core theological tenet of Christianity: God never fails, but you do.

The ancient Greek word for sin is *hamartano*, which means *to miss*, as in a target with an arrow or an animal with a spear—it's used both literally and metaphorically in ancient literature. In Greek mythology, *hamartano* is the tragic flaw carried by every hero. For Achilles, it's the vulnerable heel by which his mother, Thetis, held him when she dipped the rest of him in the River Styx. For Oedipus, it's hubris. *Nota bene*, Sophocles doesn't fault Oedipus for this flaw; Oedipus is blind to his flaw, as all humans are, blindness that goes from metaphorical to literal when Oedipus gouges his own eyes out.

For Plato, *hamartano* is the defective nature of all humans. Aristotle defines it as missing the target of virtue, the desired goal for every human—whether by accident or intent is immaterial. In his handbook on ethics, Aristotle says that virtue is the mean, the center between two extremes; *hamartano* is falling to one side or the other, rolling the bowling ball into the gutter and missing the pins.

The writers of the New Testament redefined it to mean outright hostility toward God. Guilt was the Christian innovation in the concept of *hamartano*. In the moral universe of the New Testament, we are agents, capable of deciding for ourselves about doing the right thing or the wrong, no longer puppets of the gods on Mt. Olympus. This is the world in which I was brought up and, if anything, I embraced too tightly.

In general, we're obsessed with success and frightened of failure. The market for ACT and SAT tutoring is $12 billion per year. Stories abound of parents lobbying college professors to give their kids better grades, or of assaulting a Little League umpire because a call didn't go their way. French physician René Leriche wrote, "Every surgeon carries within himself a small cemetery, where from time to time he goes to pray—a place of bitterness and regret, where he must look for an explanation for his failures."[1] Nevertheless, every surgeon also carries millions of dollars of malpractice insurance. It seems the only place we celebrate failure is on social media: videos of dads falling off ladders, boats sinking, bridesmaids passing out.

Consider farming. For hundreds of generations, our ancestors planted crops and prayed for adequate rain, for ample sunshine, for the locusts to stay away. In spite of their prayers, crops failed, often for years at a time. Famine was a common experience for the ancients, and some of the Bible's greatest dramas play out against its backdrop. Joseph was in prison when he interpreted Pharaoh's dream about seven fat cows eating seven lean ones as a prediction of famine. Consequently promoted to vizier, he stocked the granaries during the seven bountiful years, made the Pharaoh a fortune during the famine, and then rescued the Hebrew people.

The migration drama in the book of Ruth begins with the line, "In the days when the judges ruled, there was famine in the land." A couple centuries later, Israel's greatest king, David, asked his prophet, Samuel, why they were in the midst of a three-year famine. The Lord told Samuel that the Hebrews were paying the price for the sins of their former king, Saul. So David hanged seven of Saul's descendants in atonement, and the famine ended.

The Bible's prophetic, poetic, and apocalyptic books are rife with dire prophecies of famine: "When he opened the fourth seal, I heard the voice of the fourth living creature call out, 'Come!' I looked and there was a pale green horse! Its rider's name was Death, and Hades followed with him; they were given authority over a fourth of the earth, to kill with sword, famine, and pestilence, and by the wild animals of the earth."[2] Crop failure consumed the ancient imagination.

These days we walk into the store and get bent out of shape if the avocados aren't ripe. Farmers drive quarter-million dollar tractors that plant in intervals determined by GPS satellites. And if they have a bad year, the U.S. government insures them against crop failure. Although it still haunts other parts of the world, famine is unknown to us in the United States.

In seminary, I was required to take an ethics class, the subject matter of which hovered mainly in the clouds of abstraction and theory. But at least we talked about ethics. After seminary that conversation ended. In my three years of living and working on an Indian reservation, we avoided discussing the ethics of van loads of white kids arriving every week to do "mission work." And when I became a pastor at a church, our staff meetings focused on enforcing the laminated coffee policy posted in the kitchen and debating whether the volunteer ushers were adequately trained in the use of the emergency defibrillator. We did not discuss the ethics of pastoral care or church growth. I did once accuse another pastor on staff of being unethical. I'd found a bulletin in the copy machine for a liturgy of marriage dissolution. I confronted him and accused him of blessing a failure. He assured me that's exactly what he was doing. I was young and insolent, and in denial about my own failing marriage.

One aspect of hunting that I appreciate, given my experience in church, is the interest in ethics. Regulations come out each August that set the rules for fall hunting and trapping, and they're followed six months later by regs for the fishing season. These are the letters of the law set by departments of natural resources and of fish and wildlife, the twentieth century version of Hubertus's stag, and enforced by game wardens and conservation officers.

But failure is not really covered in the regs, and failure is a big part of life in wild places. We wound animals, but not always fatally. Every angler has released a fish back into the lake after extracting a swallowed hook, only to see the fish floating belly-up a few minutes later. And I can't count the times I've dropped a leg on a pheasant: shot too low, breaking one or both legs of the bird, and watched it fly away with dangling, useless limbs—its landing place will be its final resting place. While it hasn't (yet) happened to me, most deer hunters have misplaced a shot and spent a day or two tracking a wounded deer. Maybe they don't find it, or maybe they do and it's been ravaged by coyotes or a wolf; an animal, wounded by a human, rendered helpless against another predator.

In these cases, our failures cause suffering.

I carry my failures around with me, the mistakes I made, both in the marriage and getting out of it, and I can recount them in exacting detail: the time that the kids caught me with an item of their mother's that I'd sworn I didn't have; my rage when I had to wait at the curb of her house for the kids to come out; the friendships lost because no one really wanted to hear me recount my misfortune again.

I had entered adulthood unprepared for failure, a son of entitlement. My mother reinforced the you-can-do-anything-you-set-out-to-do lesson almost daily, and I believed it. When I was admitted to an Ivy League university, God was affirming my mother's prophecies. Like so many Christians, I attributed minor setbacks to God having other plans for me. I had moments of self-doubt, but my general outlook was that God had a plan for me, a good plan. In the words of the Prophet Jeremiah and innumerable needlepointed pillows, "For surely I know the plans I have for you, says the Lord, plans for your welfare and not for harm, to give you a future with hope."

Then, in late July 2008, my friend Mark walked out of my house, slumped into the passenger seat of my car, put his hand on my knee, and said, "Brother, your marriage is over." He'd flown to Minnesota on a peacekeeping mission to save our union. He and I stayed at my parents' house as he made sorties into the conflict zone, trying to broker peace. I stood in the backyard, not allowed to enter my own home, and watched the kids bounce on the trampoline. Mark sat inside, listening to my wife and trying to chart a way forward. After his final attempt at a diplomatic solution, he admitted defeat. He advised surrender.

It felt like a bag of wet sand had landed on my sternum. I had not honestly considered the possibility that we wouldn't be able to stay married, to remain an intact family.

Even in the conflagration of litigation that followed, I fought as though I could win. As a result, I failed at failing. I read reports criticizing my parenting or questioning my mental health as indictments to be fought, not lessons to be learned. Friends slid away from me, and I didn't consider that maybe they were weary of me and my troubles. Motions were denied and judges lectured us from the bench about putting the kids first, but I took those as more reasons to fight. I had failed at marriage, but I wasn't going to fail at divorce.

But divorce, I came to learn, is born in failure.

Looking for resources to deal with my failure, I turned to Emil Cioran, the philosopher of failure. Cioran lived through the thick of the twentieth century, a son of Romania who settled in Paris. His first book, *On the Heights of Despair*, was written in the midst of a seven-year bout of insomnia and depression when he was 24. He didn't write systematically, but aphoristically and with great wit, in spite of the darkness of his subject matter. By all accounts he was a happy misanthrope who lived at the edge of poverty and turned down all of the awards and accolades offered him by French intellectual society. He loved losers and considered successful people charlatans who look the same, talk the same, and wrap themselves in success in order to hide from the truth: the nature of our existence is utterly absurd and wallpapered with failure.

Cioran was in the lineage of the ancient Gnostics, a group that antagonized the early Christian church. The Gnostics looked around at our imperfect world and the absurdities built into it—that we have to consume plants and animals in order to live, for instance—and concluded that this could not have been the work of One Perfect Creator. Instead, the world must be the creation of an imperfect god or gods. Even if Cioran didn't embrace Gnostics' cosmology, he at least appreciated their realism about the state of affairs in which we find ourselves, and he often wrote glowingly about them.

Freed from the need to write theodicy, to make *apologiae* for God and attribute everything wrong with the world to sin, Cioran could reflect on the nature of the cosmos, not as some idealized, religious version of the world as it should be, but as it actually is. And failure, he found, is the most common characteristic across all planes of existence, from the cosmic (stars consuming planets) to the societal (nation-states warring and collapsing) to the personal. He was well-acquainted with failure, having backed a fascist government in his homeland as a young man—he'd even expressed admiration for Hitler. But instead of trying to scrub his youthful indiscretions from the public eye, he returned to them, turning them over in his mind, addressing them occasionally in his writings and in letters to his brother. Investigating his own failures was the key that unlocked the door to true self-understanding:

> This is how we recognize the man who has tendencies toward an inner quest: he will set failure above any success, he will even seek it out, unconsciously, of course. This is because failure, always *essential*, reveals us to ourselves, permits us to see ourselves as God sees us, whereas success distances us from what is most inward in ourselves and indeed in everything.[3]

It's trite but true: we learn from our failures. Buddhist author Pema Chodron writes that "mistakes are the portal to creativity, to learning something new, to having a fresh look on things."[4] She's right, but it's more than that. Failure is ontological, it's *who we are*. We're made of star-stuff, grit from an incomprehensibly absurd universe. Therefore, we should aim the ship at the rocks; it's going to hit them anyway, so we may as well be fully conscious when they rip open the hull and water pours in.

For a time, I wanted to erase my failure from our collective memory bank (aka, the internet). Companies offer that service: they could push my past peccadilloes down in the search engine results, burying my failures in an algorithm. But what would that accomplish? Convince the world that I didn't fail at marriage? That my career didn't crash and burn? That I am failure-proof?

Cioran wrote that only "in failure, in the greatness of a catastrophe, can you know someone."[5] That includes knowing myself, because admitting failure requires honesty about my own predicament. The more successful I was, the more inured I became to the absurdity of life. I convinced myself that salvation was possible, through work and wealth and social status.

But the one who embraces failure can become, like Cioran, *un pessimiste joyeux,* a joyful pessimist.

Now I think that's why God lured me into outdoors life, because the woods are rife with failure. Every toppled tree testifies to its own failure to withstand one storm or another. The picked-clean ribcage of a deer proclaims its failure to escape a predator.

Failure isn't hidden in the wilderness. If you look, it's everywhere, in the messiness and chaos, in the struggles to survive. And when I, as a human animal, venture into the wilderness, my own failures pile up: failure to find a portage for the canoes as a storm approaches and darkness bears down; failure to hit the deer I'm aiming at; failure to get that huge northern pike from the lake into the boat. Take, for example, something as mundane as tripping and falling: if I trip walking through the mall, people gasp and rush to my aid, so out of place is that foible in the midst of civilization. But when I trip on a hike or a hunt, it's part of the deal, at most cause for a chuckle. When I fail to get a fire going because there's no dry wood to be found, what am I going to do? Get mad at the forest? Rage at the rain? In the wild places, my failures become trivial, subsumed into an environment of broken branches and biotic compost. In that context, my failure takes on a new hue, not so dark, not so bleak. Maybe even a bit *joyeux.*

The leopard, one of the most effective predators in the world, is successful at killing its prey about one-third of the time, which I remind myself when I miss a shot. If I didn't fail, I wouldn't keep going back. Each failure carries the seed of its own redemption, because no failure—even death—is final. Every failure holds a promise and a lesson, reveals something that I didn't previously see, even reveals something about the nature of the cosmos: the carbon of which we're made comes from a generation of stars that lived and died billions of years ago.

The bigger the failure, the bigger the revelation. Based on the Gospel accounts, it's pretty clear that, in the moment, Jesus' followers considered the last few days of his life a failure. They'd entered Jerusalem at his side as crowds cheered and carpeted his path with palms. Jesus condemned the marketplace of sacrificial animals, which both drew the ire of the Temple leaders and further convinced his disciples that he was on the verge of political victory. But then a tornado of events—kiss, arrest, flogging, interrogation—swept through their little fellowship, and within hours of sitting with him at dinner, they were standing at the foot of a cross. Their erstwhile leader hung naked, humiliated, and dying—a failure by any measure. Only in retrospect, as they gathered in various collections and recounted his sayings and miracles, did they realize that his failure was his victory, making the cross the most improbable religious symbol in history.

Which is why I now see the decade of my forties as the crucible of my life. I tried so hard for so long to stave off failure. Only when it totally overwhelmed me, crushed me, pinned me to the mat, did I accept it. And accepting it as core to my very being allowed me to move forward. Both scarlet letter and stigmata, my failure is my shame and my salvation.

I'm in the San Juan Mountains of southwest Colorado on my first elk hunt. Seth, my friend from earlier, churchier days, and her partner, Tony, are my hosts and guides. They live in two reclaimed miners' shacks that have been stitched together. My billet, a futon not six feet from their bed, is piled high with heavy wool blankets because, as Seth tells me, they like it cold. Their kitchen, which she lovingly calls the Apothecary, boasts jars and bottles in various stages of fermentation, and scores of herbs, hanging and drying.

Reared in a fundamentalist family, Seth grew up being home-schooled at her family's kitchen table. A non-negotiable moral code about what was right and what was wrong, good and bad, black and white, male and female, guided the family. Seth then matriculated into a fundamentalist college in South Dakota, and the prairie landscape captivated her.

She started pursuing deeper questions about herself and her faith not because she thought Christianity was weak but because she considered it strong enough to handle the challenges she threw at it. Along the way, she embraced some changes in herself: Sara Beth Donovan became Seth Siobhan O'Donovan. Straight became queer. Monogamous became polyamorous. And Christian became—something more than Christian, a polyglot spirituality that embraces the "New Age" beliefs and practices I'd preached against in my younger days, and that Seth simply refers to as "woo-woo."

Since I'd last seen Seth, she had worked in several high-profile restaurants, including a two-year stint at the French Laundry, north of San Francisco. But the wild mountains pulled her back to Colorado, and she shifted from the finest dining to butchering her own goats, fermenting wild vinegars, drying herbs, concocting tinctures. Currently Seth is: in an apprenticeship with an herbologist, in training to become a falconer, taking classes toward becoming an EMT, and on the volunteer fire department, all in addition to her full-time job managing a small mountain resort.

As I sit in one of the two chairs in their shack, she gives me a tour of the Apothecary: a taste of spruce vinegar, a sip of yarrow tea, a sniff of dried nettles, a soupçon of porcini mushroom powder, each lovingly harvested by Seth and Tony from roadside ditches and high mountain meadows.

She tells me that she asks every plant's permission before she picks it.

Snarkily, I ask if any have said no.

Yes, she assures me that some have. I wonder aloud if the plants' wordless answers are similar to what our parents and Sunday school teachers taught us: that God answers us, but often without words. Yes, she nods, it's the same.

I've never hunted elk before, and this area of Colorado is one of the few places in the country that sells over-the-counter tags to non-resident hunters. When I pulled off of the state highway, I rolled up a hairy switchback road toward a high meadow, then caught the gravel road that led me down the other side of the pass. As I drove past trailheads, each was cluttered with half-a-dozen pickups, hunters in blaze orange, and trailers hauling either horses or four-wheelers. They're all here to hunt, too, in spite of the odds: the success rate in this unit for bagging a bull elk is a sobering 13.2 percent.

Notwithstanding that dismal probability, Seth and Tony exude optimism. They know these mountains, they've seen lots of elk, and they assure me that we'll find some. In my own hubris, I assume that I'm among the 13.2 percent best hunters in the area.

On the first two days, Tony and I scout. Day one, we hike a steep mountain trail, ascending over 2,000 feet of elevation through spruce forest, hopscotching mountain streams. We hear the bugle call of a male elk and excitedly scramble upward, only to come upon a wall tent replete with propane tanks, a heater, and a grill. Two hunters emerge from the tent flap, decked out in expensive gear. They tell us that they came up the same trail we did, only they rode on horses provided by a guide. That guide also set up their bivouac and provided them enough food for 10 days. In short, they'd claimed this mountainside and the plateau above. Tony and I dejectedly descend.

Abandoning that plan, on day two we drive back up to the high meadow I'd traversed on my arrival. We hike for an hour across open grass pasture and then turn into a 500-acre plot of dark timber. For several hours we follow elk trails. I pick up elk scat, testing its warmth. By the time we hike out at dusk, we feel confident that elk hide out in these woods, so the next afternoon we return with Seth and set up at the edge of a small meadow crisscrossed by tracks. We see no elk that night. But as we sit, Seth asks me whether I have any rituals when I shoot an animal. I tell her that I don't. She tells me that she sings. Death is such a struggle, she says, similar to birthing. The first time she butchered a goat, she just naturally started to sing. "Singing and mantras and hymns are instruments to help us move through those times," she says. "They reassure us and calm us and also encourage us." She felt like that goat needed a song, and now she sings to every animal she slaughters.

For the next two days, we set up over a small, muddy pond. I'd stuck my head over a hillock and seen three elk coming down an aspen stand, and the tracks around the water indicate that the elk use it for drinking and wallowing. Plus, a friend of mine who's shot several elk gave me some advice before my trip: no water, no elk.

But even with water, no elk.

On my last evening in Colorado, over a whiskey, we catch up on life, talking about the changes wrought in both of us in the decade since we'd seen one another. I ask Seth if being queer means she hunts differently than I do. She tells me that being queer has changed how she thinks of binaries. It's not that binaries don't exist—male and female, teacher and student, plant and animal, success and failure, life and death—it's that she no longer sees them as standing in opposition to one another. It's why she sits down next to a nettle and asks, "Can I harvest you?" Because that nettle exists on a continuum that also includes Seth.

Then she says that while we were sitting that morning, she meditated on the fact that we were actively trying to kill our Brother Elk. "I just thought about this all morning," she says. "I was sitting there trying to call Brother Elk to us so that we could kill him."

Her voice catches in her throat. I blink back tears.

For my final hunt, we decide to stalk instead of sit. We climb a mountainside, ford drainages, and scramble over deadfalls. We roust two elk from their beds, and they gallop away. Steam rises from where they'd been sleeping, their musk hangs in the air. We come across more fresh tracks and scat and even startle an elk cow, but we never see a bull. I'll be driving home with empty coolers.

In spite of this, the hunt was a success. Stated more accurately, the failure *was* the success.

I deliberately undertook an endeavor with a 13.2 percent success rate. I drove 44 hours round trip and dropped a thousand bucks. I learned a lot about elk hunting. I learned from Seth. I learned about myself.

Before I leave for the drive home, Seth tells me: "You put yourself up against a force that matched you, a thousand-pound beast that's smart and fast and knows these mountains better than you. This time, Brother Elk bested you."[6]

7

Risk

This is at bottom the only courage that is demanded of us: to have courage for the most strange, the most singular and the most inexplicable that we may encounter. That mankind has in this sense been cowardly has done life endless harm: the experiences that are called 'visions,' the whole so-called 'spirit world,' death, all those things that are so closely akin to us, have by daily parrying been so crowded out of life that the senses with which we could have grasped them are atrophied. To say nothing of God.

—Rainer Maria Rilke, *Letters to a Young Poet*

DIVORCED, BROKE, AND FORECLOSED UPON, I TRIED TO MAKE memories with the kids every-Tuesday-and-every-other-weekend-and-alternating-holidays, which included Memorial Day weekend, 2012. I bought a coupon for half-off a "camper cabin" at the end of the Gunflint Trail in way-northern Minnesota. No running water, no sheets on the bed, no toilet—it's all I could afford. But the deal included a half-day rental of a fishing boat with an outboard motor, which I hoped would be the highlight of the trip.

We drove six hours north in the rain, fell asleep to the sound of rain on the cabin roof, and woke to more rain. Mounds of dirt around the newly constructed cabins had metamorphosed to rivers of mud, which we forded to the communal bathroom. The kids were 12, 10, and 7. We spent most of the first day reading books, confined to the tiny cabin by a chill drizzle. We ate cold cereal for breakfast and soggy sandwiches for lunch, and I attempted in vain to light charcoal on the cabin's grill for dinner. Instead we drove to Trail Center Lodge for burgers and milkshakes.

The next day the weather broke, so we grabbed our fishing gear, hiked down the hill to the docks, and claimed our boat. The lodge is at the west end of Gunflint Lake, a long sweep of water that runs east-west. After getting some advice from other anglers who were pushing off, we puttered east, trolling for fish of any kind. I sat in the stern, a hand on the tiller, while the kids hung lines over the gunwales. At some point, Aidan hooked into a big one, and I awkwardly reached to help him net the fish while also trying to keep the boat pointed into the wind, which was picking up. Cheers of elation erupted when we got the fish in the boat: a three-and-a-half pound lake trout. A beast.

"Who wants to go to Canada?" I asked, pointing north across the narrows. "It's right over there." More cheers. I turned the boat north and throttled up the motor. On the far shore of Gunflint Lake the kids climbed out onto a rock. I snapped a photo and congratulated them on being international travelers.

As the kids got back into the boat, I noticed the clouds overhead: low enough to touch, it seemed, and racing across the sky. Unusually, they moved from east to west, giving the waves a seven-mile runway down the lake to pick up steam. Then the rain started, horizontal, huge drops pelting us like miniature water balloons exploding on our faces. The storm was upon us before I knew what was happening.

I tried pointing the boat south, but the first wave that hit the port side almost capsized us. I wrestled with the tiller, turning us east into the whitecaps. I shouted over the wind and rain for the kids to sit three abreast on the middle bench and hang on to one another. The dead trout sloshed around the deck in the expanding pool of water.

When the bow crested a swell, the wind batted the boat sideways, and breakers again threatened to surmount the port side. I shouted at Tanner to move forward—"We need weight in the bow!" He looked back at me with distress etched on his face. On all fours, he crawled to the front bench, scrambled onto it, and braced himself by grabbing the bow with both hands. Aidan and Lily bounced on the middle bench with each wave, laughing, blissfully unaware of the severity of our predicament.

I couldn't see more than 20 feet in front of us. I steered the boat straight into the wind. I hoped we were going east-south-east, but I had no way of knowing, since I could see no landmarks and had no compass, and we were 30 miles from a cell phone tower. We mounted each wave and violently slapped down on the other side. Mid-wave, the outboard motor's prop came out of the water and cavitated, suffocating on air. If the motor died, we'd be in real trouble. I rotated the tiller handle counterclockwise, throttling down—if I spun it too far, I'd kill the engine. I found a rhythm, throttling up when we climbed a wave, throttling down when we descended the other side.

Seeing a generous trough between waves, I pulled the tiller hard to port, swinging the boat around. Now we were going with the wind, the gale astern. Good news: we made better progress and the pitching was less violent. Bad news: the occasional rogue wave came over the transom. The water in the boat was ankle-deep. Lightning flashed, followed too closely by teeth-rattling thunder.

I zigged and zagged our way across the lake: into the wind, then with the wind. I figured that we'd eventually reach the south shore, where I'd beach the boat and find shelter. But then, after I-don't-know-how-long, Tanner shouted that he saw something. The end of a dock came into view, then we saw our boat's siblings, rocking in their slips. Somehow we'd emerged from the squall at the exact right spot.

I clumsily docked the boat and we scrambled out, bedraggled and soaked. My body shuddered with cold, and with the terror that only really hit me when we were safely on shore. But the kids—the kids were gleeful. For them it had been an adventure to rival any amusement park ride. Aidan giddily held up his trout and asked if we could cook it for dinner. We did, and we agreed it was the best fish we'd ever eaten.

That night as I lay awake, images of an upturned boat and three children gasping for air tormented me, along with voices in my head telling me what a terrible father I am.

Danger is in the eye of the beholder. Getting caught in a squall will seem the height of unnecessary risk to some, a banal boat trip to others.

For the most part, other species do a much better job of gauging risk than we do. On a recent hunting trip, I drove toward a field with hundreds of pheasants scratching for grain. Sensing the danger of an approaching predator, they took flight en masse before I could even put the truck's transmission in park. I've flushed any number of species out of their safe havens in cattail sloughs or high brome grass: deer, rabbits, hares, coyotes, foxes, possums, badgers, and more. Anyone who's hunted turkeys knows that the most innocent twig snap will send a tom running. Animals—prey animals in particular—have a sixth sense for danger.

But homo sapiens have lost much of our ability to judge danger—or worse, we misjudge it. For example, it's well established that we're far less likely to die in a plane crash than a car wreck—Americans have a 1-in-7,178 chance of dying in a plane crash and a 1-in-98 chance of dying in an automobile crash—yet aerophobia is far more common than amaxophobia. We also overestimate deaths by fire and earthquakes, and underestimate deaths by diabetes and drowning. Social theorists blame our faulty perception of risk on "availability bias," our tendency to rely on immediate and vivid memories rather than data and general trends when making judgments and decisions.

Availability bias was once important, a significant evolutionary trait, because our ancestors encountered risk in ways that we no longer do. Their world was a dangerous place, full of inexplicable ailments. People dropped dead for no apparent reason; the sky poured forth terrific storms; sometimes the earth quaked, or it spouted lava that incinerated everything in its path. Awareness of acute dangers kept our forebears alive: after you see a tiger eat your best friend, you tend to avoid tigers. But also, their bodies regularly betrayed them, and, unable to see viruses and bacteria and cancerous cells, they blamed their ailments on evil spirits and unbalanced humors.

In addition to defending themselves physically, the ancients mitigated risk though sacrifices and prayers, dances and rituals and gifts to the gods—through religion. Appeasing and appealing to the gods lessened the ever-present danger in the world.[1] The refrain of the childhood prayer, "and if I die before I wake," holds both the fear of inexplicable death and the promise of a God who's paying attention, as does the more formal Compline prayer of the Anglicans: "Save us, O Lord, while waking, and guard us while sleeping, that . . . asleep we may rest in peace."

But we don't experience nearly the danger that our ancestors did. Our life expectancy is over twice what it was just 200 years ago—meaning those archaic prayers ring a bit hollow since most of us don't go to sleep worried that we might not wake up in the morning. Today, science is the framework by which we understand the forces that threaten us: modern medicine explains all and cures most of the ailments that killed our ancestors; meteorologists warn us of oncoming storms; geologists excise the mystery from earthquakes and volcanoes.

In fact, we are so insulated from true danger that we have a hard time judging actual risk, which, ironically, cripples us. A related evolutionary trait that's outlived its usefulness is our desire to protect our offspring. We wrap them in metaphorical bubble wrap, guarding them against injury and disappointment. But this tendency has the counterintuitive effect of increasing their anxiety, as seen in the skyrocketing rates of teen depression, self-harm, and suicide.

Recently, my wife Courtney has been afflicted by allergies, waking up many times each night with fits of sneezing. She went to an allergist, who administered a series of pricks of allergens to her back. Her skin lit up like a Christmas tree. "Basically, you're allergic to everything," the doctor told her—trees, grasses, dust, pets. Based on her results, the doctor mixed up a cocktail of everything she's allergic to, and for a year she's getting a weekly injection with a tiny amount of each allergen. The cure is exposure.

If we want kids who are independent, resilient, and spiritually strong, we need to expose them to some peril, because it turns out that their brains are hungry for it. In studies, adolescents show a couple of unique and related neurological traits based in the plasticity of their brains: first, the prefrontal cortex, associated with long-term planning and self-control, is still forming; and second, the ventral striatum, associated with responding to reward, is firing at a high rate. As a result, more than children or adults, teenagers exhibit a "higher tolerance for the unknown."[2] This is another evolutionary trait. When lifespans were shorter, "adolescents needed to explore their world to find food and mates."[3] For cave-teens to procreate, they needed to leave mom and dad's cave and venture out into the wider world, which meant risk.

Relative to the cave-teens, most teenagers today live in a world that's much less risky. But their brains haven't evolved quite as quickly as civilization. Adolescents seek out risky behavior like driving too fast or experimenting with drugs because their brains are on the hunt for the rush of the risk-reward cycle.

I didn't know that science when I was a youth pastor. I just knew intuitively, and from my own experience of being a teenager, that the kids in my youth group would benefit from some adventure and risk. That's why we did trust falls and high ropes courses and rode roller coasters. The best example of this was a trip I led with a handful of 18-year-old guys who'd just graduated from high school. We drove the church van to Colorado and camped in the outback. Each day, we had a different adventure: we skied at Arapahoe Basin (in shorts on July 4); we rappelled down a 400-foot rock face; we mountain biked around Rampart Reservoir; we summited three 14,000-foot peaks—Mts. Democrat, Lincoln, and Bross—in a day.

The highlight of the trip was the final adventure, when we rafted down the whitewater rapids of the Arkansas River. These guys had rafted the Arkansas with me previously, when I'd brought their confirmation class to Colorado three years earlier. But none of us had rafted the section that runs through the Royal Gorge. One of the roughest stretches of raftable water in the world, the Gorge is Class V, "expert" on the six-class scale of rapids (Class VI being "extreme and exploratory" and not open to commercial rafts).

To prepare us for our afternoon trip down the Gorge, our guide made us jump out of the raft in the morning and swim through Satan's Suckhole, a Class III. He steered the raft alongside our bobbing heads, teaching us to float feet first with our arms across our chests and our feet pointed downstream to deflect boulders in our path. "If you get maytagged"—stuck in a washing-machine-like whirlpool—"don't fight it. The rapid will eventually spit you out," he advised. "And do not try to stand up!"

We beached the raft at noon and ate lunch out of a cooler that had been bungied in the boat. The guide told us that the Gorge had been closed the week before due to high water levels, and the week before that a 12-year-old girl died. She fell out of her raft and made the fatal mistake of standing up—her foot got trapped between two rocks, and the force of the current pushed her face-first into the water where she drowned. The guys ate in silence, sitting on the shore with the deafening sound of the river rushing past us at 2,000 cubic feet per second—a million gallons every minute. The Gorge was just around the next bend. Our guide talked us through the rapids we'd be facing: Pumphouse, Sledgehammer, Car Crash Hole, Wall Slammer, Fishbowl, and Boat Eater.

Then he instructed us: if you fall out of the raft, do not under any circumstances swim to either shore—one side has jagged rocks, and the other has rods of rebar from an old railroad. "Just go with the current," he said. "One of the other rafts will pick you out of the water, but not until you're out of the Gorge."

He unclipped a string of helmets that had been in the raft all morning and handed them out.

I noticed one of the guys silently crying, then another. They'd been tough all week, conquering challenge after challenge, but now they were afraid.

We survived the Gorge. The ride was exhilarating. And probably not all that dangerous—the guide confided in me later that he'd run the Gorge on a boogie board the week that it was closed, so the perceived risk was higher than the actual risk. Nevertheless, that afternoon of whitewater rafting affected each of us deeply. Back at camp around the fire, more tears flowed as the young men opened up about their fears, their relationships with their dads, and what kind of dads they wanted to be. In my two decades as a youth pastor, it was the most intense, intimate, vulnerable discussion I ever led, made possible by six miles of whitewater—made possible by exposing them to risk.

What's good for the gosling is good for the goose: adults also benefit from being exposed to risk in the wilderness. The neural circuits in our brains fall into two categories, excitatory and inhibitory, the former outnumbering the latter by about two-to-one. The inhibitory cells are under-active in adolescence, but they grow into their role as the brain's traffic cops as we age, allowing us regulate our behavior and exhibit self-control. Deep learning happens when the excitatory neurons are firing more liberally, without the guard rails of the inhibitory cells. Even as adults, learning is often associated with risk-taking.[4]

Or consider a couple of chemicals in the brain. Serotonin is an inhibitory neurotransmitter that affects our moods, sexual desires, and appetites. Dopamine, another neurotransmitter, sends signals of pleasure—many illicit drugs, for instance, trigger the release of dopamine, which can lead to abuse and addiction. And the software developers behind all of the most popular social media sites have admitted that their algorithms and notifications were built to reward users with tiny dopamine hits, like rats hitting a lever to get a food pellet. These artificial stimulants and online "communities" are taking advantage of dopamine's important evolutionary function in our brains: the risk-reward mechanism. We will take risks if there's a potential reward, and the reward is the feeling of pleasure that washes through our brains when dopamine is released.[5] And, like excitatory cells, dopamine is associated with our ability to learn.

When I guide a group of adults on a canoe trip into the Boundary Waters Canoe Area, I can almost smell the dopamine levels increasing as we drive north on I-35. We stop for lunch in Duluth—without fail at Northern Waters Smoke Haus. For months I've fielded their questions via text and email, but as we sit at picnic tables and eat gravlax sandwiches, they come fast: How bad will the bugs be? What if I can't keep up with the group? What about bears!?! After driving a couple more hours along the north shore of Lake Superior, we arrive in Grand Marais. We grab a beer at Voyageur Brewing and fishing licenses at Buck's Hardware.

Then, before we drive up the Gunflint Trail, which is joyously void of cell phone reception, I tell everyone to call their loved ones and say goodbye—we'll be out-of-range for the next six days. Bidding farewell like this used to be common. Our forebears left for seasons or years at a time, to hunt or to war, on pilgrimages or train trips or sea voyages; they'd send letters that would take months to arrive. But now we've become accustomed to being in-touch all the time, so these goodbye phone calls in the brewery parking lot are fraught with emotion.

We head up the Trail and spend a night at the outfitter's, packing gear and sleeping on bunks. We're up early the next morning and rattling up the Trail in a decommissioned church van.

Standing at the launch at the south end of the strait that will lead us into Saganaga Lake, canoes half in water and half on shore, paddles in hand, the nervous energy is palpable—maybe not with the same intensity as the teenage boys looking into the teeth of the Gorge, but similar. The men and women I take into the wilderness tend to live urban, sedentary lives. Venturing into a wild place like the BWCA is physically riskier than anything else they do in a year, and, consequently, the rewards that await them are rich. Over six days, their backs will ache from paddling, they will struggle to light fires for cooking and warmth, they'll feel the slice of nylon straps into their shoulders as they carry 50-pound packs over rocky portages. Very likely, one of them will get sick or hurt. We'll be wet, cold, bug-bitten, blistered, exhausted, and smelly.

Recently I took a group of pastors into the BWCA. David was particularly nervous as we launched, and around the campfire at the end of the first day he confessed that he'd considered turning around about halfway into our six-hour paddle. He'd been a successful IT entrepreneur who, after selling his business, went to seminary and became a pastor. And he was stressed. He was pushing himself as hard as a pastor as he had as a businessman. This voyage was well outside his comfort zone, and he told us that his wife and children couldn't believe he was doing it. Each day, he got better at paddling and portaging, and more relaxed in the wilderness.

On our last night, sitting on a rock overlooking Sea Gull Lake, another member of the group, Chris, told David: "You said earlier that your kids never see you smile, that they always think you're so stressed. Well, you've been smiling and laughing for the last couple days." Tears filled David's eyes. He hadn't even noticed. Amidst the struggle and risk involved in a wilderness canoe trip, some knot inside of David had come loose. Shortly after the trip, he resigned his position at the church.

At the end of each canoe excursion in the BWCA, when we see that rickety old van waiting for us at the end of Sea Gull Lake, something else happens—something less in the head and more in the chest—less neurons, more pneuma. We've got more knots in our shoulders, but fewer knots in our chests.

Stepping out of our comfortable, daily routines and into a wild place, taking on challenges that involve risk, is good for us. It fires our excitatory neurotransmitters, and it releases dopamine, exactly what happened in the primitive brains of our primordial ancestors when they went out on a hunt or battled with another tribe or moved the clan through hostile territory from the summer grounds to the winter grounds. The same neurological processes that kept them alive will benefit us, if we activate them.

It makes sense that our species has collectively weeded out most of the physical risks in life, and when new risks pop up, we mitigate them as well. Vaccines and seatbelts, blood thinners and stents and chemotherapy and home security systems all reduce the risks to life. Ten thousand years ago, acquiring food by going out on a hunt was a high-risk affair with a not insignificant mortality rate, and until recently, giving birth was the most dangerous moment in a woman's life. The grocery store and the maternity ward have lessened those risks significantly.

But there's another kind of peril that may be uniquely human: a broken heart. That's a risk that evolution has not mitigated. On the contrary, our advanced rationality, our self-awareness produces that risk. Whenever we fall in love, have children, open ourselves to deep friendship, even acquire a pet, we open ourselves to the possibility—the probability—of having our hearts broken. The suffering that gutted me came not from a mountain-climbing accident or a spelunking mishap but from a broken relationship, one that held great promise at the beginning, and even produced the wonder of three children, but ended in suffering—with not physical but psychic injury. And not just for the two adults, but also for those three children.

On pheasant hunts, we go to Geddes, South Dakota because of the Lone Tree Steak House, the best restaurant for miles around. Geddes was always small, but now it's tiny. The long-since-abandoned hotel is four stories high and doesn't have a single intact window. The bank is boarded up. Hell, almost every building is boarded up.

In the middle of Main Street, surrounded by pickup trucks, sits a brown, squat metal building. The façade sports a couple of those high windows meant to let some light in but keep prying eyes out, and the front door sports a full-length Budweiser ad, a giant sticker affixed to the indoor side of the glass.

It's my son Tanner's first hunting trip with me. Ten months ago he decided to defy a court order and live with me. Like me, he's wounded, but in the divorce that precipitated all this pain, he is neither the protagonist nor antagonist; he's merely an innocent bystander, a civilian casualty, torn through with psychological shrapnel. He took a risk when he moved in full-time with Courtney and me. I have followed his lead and asked the court for full custody. It's a financial risk to fire up the litigation engine again. But the bigger risk to me is emotional—I don't know how I'll survive more hearings, more evaluations, and another potential defeat in court.

We left home just after 5:00 a.m. and he slept for all but 20 minutes of the five-and-a-half hour drive. He's tired a lot, and like so many aspects of raising kids through a brutal divorce, I can't tell if his constant exhaustion is normal for a 15-year-old or a physiological sign of our familial conflict. While he slept, I listened to Christmas music, made a couple phone calls, and thought about my life. I have yet another court date on Monday.

As we pull up to the field from the north, Larry and Craig pull up from the south. Larry shoots a Remington 870 Express pump shotgun. That's an inexpensive but solid gun. Although he can surely afford something nicer, he keeps shooting that old thing. And he rarely misses. Craig shoots a fancier gun and runs two world-class Vizslas— kinetic, muscular dogs whose taut skin looks two sizes too small.

We pull onto a gravel road across from Larry's land to scheme. This field—which we call Aurora because it's a couple miles south of Aurora Center, population 22—has three tree belts, a couple of food plots, and some grass. As we're talking, we can hear the cackling of pheasant roosters in the westernmost trees, and we immediately change our plans. Larry says, "A bird in the hand!"

Tanner and I are assigned to walk the eastern edge of the trees with Albert. Larry and Craig walk the other side of the trees. Tanner has never shot a living thing, and he's only once hit a moving target—a clay pigeon last summer at the cabin; I threw him about 50, and he hit a couple. So while I don't have high hopes of him bagging a bird on this first trip, I am hopeful that he'll get a feel for the rhythms of the hunt. And I'm just happy to get him away from the battle at home for a few days.

Within a couple minutes of walking—I'm in the trees and Tanner is in the adjacent corn field—there's an explosion of wings, cackles, and gunfire. A couple of hens come out our side, so it seems that the guys on the other side are getting all the action. The commotion lasts all of 30 seconds, and when we arrive at the other end of the tree belt, Craig tells us that about 60 pheasants took off and flew over the highway. They shot one.

After a day of hunting, Tanner and I arrive in Geddes first—Craig is having some trouble with a tire on his truck, and he stops in another town to get it patched. Tanner has fallen asleep in the car again, so I rouse him.

Walking into the Lone Tree, Tanner says, "Towns like this depress me."

Inside, a bar fronts the restaurant, and we take a seat at a table. Every stool at the bar is full of locals, old guys with pliers in leather sheaths on their belts and pocket knives clipped inside their jeans pockets. They don't take off their jackets when they take a seat at the bar, and the portly, middle-aged bartender serves them without even asking what they want. One young woman walks in, and he hands her a six-pack of Miller Lite and a pack of cigarettes. She puts money on the bar and walks out without exchanging a word with the bartender.

The Weather Channel plays on mute on a small TV over the bar; there's no music, it's eerily quiet; for sale on the counter are beef sticks, pickled pork feet in a tub of brine, and something called Red Skins for $1.25 a piece; occasionally one of the video lottery machines chirps. I order a beer for myself and a root beer for Tanner. After a sip, Tanner makes a face and says it tastes weird, so I look at the bottle. The waitress has served my 15-year-old son an alcoholic root beer. His eyes widen and we both laugh.

Larry and Craig arrive, and we walk back to the dining room. I'm especially thrilled to be here because last year we made the mistake of visiting the Lone Tree on Sunday night, and there's no salad bar on Sunday. Only on Friday and Saturday.

A plastic bowl of greens leads off the salad bar, but the rest consists of various items swimming in pools of mayonnaise: potato salad, coleslaw, another potato salad, seafood salad, bowtie pasta salad, macaroni salad, and a pea-and-bacon salad in which the peas and bacon have succumbed completely to the mayo. My plate—translucent glass in a flower pattern—is heavy with salads as I walk back to the table. I forgo the chocolate-mousse-with-mandarin-oranges salad.

Tanner gets the surf-n-turf—a steak and two fried jumbo shrimp—I get the petite cut prime rib; Larry the queen cut; Craig the king cut. For the next hour, we talk and laugh. We tell stories of past hunts, we joke about the quirks of our mutual friend Doug, and we discuss how we'll get those birds tomorrow in the trees. Larry asks Tanner about his life and what he likes in school. As though he's got a hollow leg, Tanner socks away calories.

Through it all I think: our troubles are a million miles away. Tanner and I cannot escape them at home—they're stalking us all the time. But we don't have cell phone coverage in Geddes. No service. It's a black hole out here, no reason to point transponders at this little town that time forgot. No way for anyone to get to us. We're off the grid. We can eat and talk in peace.

As we walk out to the car for the 40-minute drive back to our lodging, I ask Tanner if he wants to drive—he has his learner's permit. "No," he says, "I want to talk." At this point in his driving career, those two activities are mutually exclusive.

Something has broken open inside him, a new level of understanding—or at least a quest for understanding. He wants to vent, and he wants answers to his questions. We talk uninterrupted; he talks, mainly, and I listen. He is unfairly burdened, I think to myself. He should be able to enjoy these teen years in the comfort of our nice suburb, unfettered by existential risk. But that's not his fate. He is an involuntary participant in a vortex of litigation, mental illness, and child protection investigations.

When I asked Tanner to join me on this hunt, I did not think he would come. I figured he'd consider it, then decline. He'd cite homework or plans with friends or prep for his next debate tournament. But to my surprise, he texted me from school that he wanted to come. For six hours a day, we pound through fields and sloughs. It's cold and wet and exhausting. But it turns out that's exactly what he needs to relativize the emotional jeopardy he's in at home. His therapist helps—honestly, the kids' therapist is a hero in this story—but getting out into the wilderness is a necessary balm for his soul.

These 40 minutes are precious, and I treasure them. Once we get back to our motel, Tanner's phone and computer are both out of battery, and there's no wifi. He's in bed before 9 p.m., with Albert curled up beside him.

Jesus wandered into the wilderness around the age of 30, abandoning Joseph's workshop to discover his true calling. After being baptized by his cousin, Jesus followed the examples of Moses and Elijah and ventured alone into the desert. In the wadis, ravines, and caves of the Judean wild, he fasted. After six weeks, the Gospel writers tell us, he was famished. And it was then, at his weakest point, that his tempter, the devil, arrived and tried to flip him—another great drama set on the backdrop of a wild place. Jesus held strong in the face of both terrestrial and cosmic danger, and he emerged as the nascent messiah. Subsequently, he often retreated from the crowds to wild places, like the night he spent praying alone on a mountainside before choosing his disciples.

Nineteen centuries after Jesus, and eight decades before I lived there, poet John Neihardt visited Manderson, South Dakota. He wanted to interview someone who'd participated in the fabled Ghost Dance, the native ceremony that frightened the U.S. Army so much that they rounded up and massacred over 300 Lakota at Wounded Knee in 1890. Neihardt met with the holy man Black Elk (*Heȟáka Sápa*); Black Elk's son translated his father's words from Lakota into English, Neihardt's wife transcribed, and the resulting book, *Black Elk Speaks*, became one of the spiritual classics of the twentieth century.

Black Elk recounted several visions from his life, including his great vision at age nine, which took place at Owl Maker (*Hinhán Sága*), the highest peak of the Black Hills (*Pahá Sápa*). After reciting his life story to the Neihardts, Black Elk asked to return to the same spot, where the spirits had once escorted him to the center of the earth and showed him the sacred hoop of the world. Fifty-eight years after that vision, he cried out,

Grandfather, Great Spirit, once more behold me on earth and lean
to hear my feeble voice. You lived first, you are older than all need,
older than prayer. All things belong to you—the two-leggeds, the
four-leggeds, the wings of the air and all green things that live. You
have set the powers of the four quarters to cross each other. The good
road and the road of difficulties you have made to cross; and where
they cross, the place is holy. Day in and day out, forever, you are the
life of all things.[6]

Neihardt reports that tears flowed down Black Elk's cheeks as he
lamented that the tree at the center of the sacred hoop had never
bloomed. He'd personally witnessed the Battle of Little Bighorn and
the Massacre at Wounded Knee, he'd seen the extirpation of bison
and the subjugation of his own people. And what he wanted before he
died was to return to the wilderness and cry out to *Tunkashila Wakháŋ
Tháŋka* (Grandfather God, Great Spirit).

When I lived in Manderson, nearly a century later, young men still
climbed the butte east of town with only a blanket, pipe, and tobacco
and fasted for four days, participating in what has come to be known as
a vision quest. "It is necessary to go far away from people," Black Elk
said of such quests, like the one in which he was visited by an eagle and
a hawk and a cloud of beautiful butterflies. The eagle spoke to him, as
did the hawk, and the butterflies turned into swallows. A thunderstorm
swept across the plains, but neither rain nor hail fell on him.

Like Jesus and Black Elk, scores of mystics and medicine men and
abbas and ammas have gone far away from people and ventured alone
into the wilderness to find truth. Danger waited for them there, in the
shape of torments both physical and spiritual—so scarred was John of
Lycopolis, a Desert Father in the fourth century, from the assaults of
the demons that co-habited his cave that he inspired many who were
living in despair to repent of their sins and live virtuous lives.[7] John,
Jesus, and Black Elk emerged from the wilderness, not unscathed, but
with a clear vision and sense of purpose.

Tanner and I did, too.

And three weeks later, the court awarded me sole custody.

8

Meat

Mortality is almost no one's favorite subject, save for funeral directors, casket makers, pathologists, homicide detectives, and a few especially lachrymose ministers and priests. Hunting and fishing involve trip-hammering our fellow creatures into eternity. . . . If there is a virtue in distancing yourself from what you eat, I do not perceive it.

—Jim Harrison, "A New Map of the Sacred Territory"

A DEER DOESN'T HAVE FRONT SHOULDER JOINTS. IT'S ODD. THE humerus doesn't connect to the scapula in a socket like it does in the back hips—or in human shoulders, for that matter. Instead, connective tissue—cartilage and silverskin—bridge the opposing muscles like layered sheaves of paper, allowing the leg to pivot without a fulcrum.

Separating a front leg from the rest of a deer resides in my imagination as pure sense-memory. Skinned and hung for a couple days, the doe has taken on a darkened hue, her muscles' moisture wicked away by the cold November wind. I prefer to hang deer by the head, but for the purpose of carving off a front leg, hanging by a gambrel through its backward-facing knees is better. Hoisting her onto the tailgate of a pickup works, too. Press the rigor-mortised leg out and slide a sharp knife in: gentle strokes, lightly touched, the blade glides between the muscles, as if the connecting cartilage is pulling the blade, welcoming the cuts, inviting the separation. A light crackle sounds as the slightly frozen tissue tears ahead of the knife. I slice, then push the leg away, my hand around her ankle. The rift continues in rhythm: slice, push, slice, push.

The weight of the leg grows in my hand as the sinews release their grip. I carefully slip the knife blade between her beautifully striated muscle groups, careful not to nick either side. The breach complete, her leg and shoulder fall from her body. I need two hands to hold it. It's part of neither her nor me at this point, but what was part of her will become part of me.

And with that, the object before me has changed from creature to food. When I shot her and watched her die, she was all creature. I felt her death. Then I slit open her belly from throat to genitals, reached into an elbow-deep pool of her blood, and removed her innards. I hefted her still-warm, still-malleable corpse onto the back of the truck.

Hanging her and flaying her, she was still creaturely. But something happens here, during the butchery: she crosses a threshold, metamorphosing from one category to another: from animal to meat.

Months later, I'll pull that vacuum-sealed, bone-in shoulder roast from the freezer, thaw it, sprinkle the muscle with spices and flour, then I'll sear it on all sides in spitting-hot olive oil. Remove the roast from the pot. Drop in onions and carrots and celery, then garlic, which will release their fragrances as they soften. A splash of white wine and pheasant stock to deglaze the tastiest bits, charred to the bottom of the pot. Then back in goes the roast, along with two sprigs of rosemary, a couple bay leaves, and more stock. Heft the heavy-lidded pot into the oven for a long, slow braise. When it emerges hours later, the meat melts like butter before knife and tooth. As they chew, my diners ooh and ahh and tell me they've never tasted such good venison and they used to hate venison and this isn't gamey at all and can they have the recipe.

But now, standing at the back of my truck, it's just become venison. A couple minutes ago, she was still deer. She didn't transmogrify on her own—this sentence cannot be rendered in the passive voice. *I* am the subject of the sentence: Tony killed her. Tony butchered her. Tony converted her from deer to venison.

I did this by removing, bit by bit, what made her deer. As I removed each bit, her deerness ebbed—I stripped her of her deerness. Looking at a skinned deer, hanging from a tree, is to behold an object in a liminal state. The act of butchering represents the doorway. I disassemble the carcass, expunging the last of her deerness. I push her over the line from animal to protein, from fauna to food, from *her* to *it*. She was a whole, a sum of her parts: head, neck, back, legs, hide, hooves. Now it sits in piles, laid out in groups, going by names not of body parts but of cuts: tenderloin, backstrap, sirloin, roast, shank.

Humans have been doing what I'm doing for a very, very long time. But maybe not forever. The following account, from the mythopoetic tale of the world's creation in Genesis, implies that the first generation of creatures, humans included, were herbivores:

> God said, "See, I have given you every plant yielding seed that is upon the face of all the earth, and every tree with seed in its fruit; you shall have them for food. And to every beast of the earth, and to every bird of the air, and to everything that creeps on the earth, everything that has the breath of life, I have given every green plant for food." And it was so. God saw everything that he had made, and indeed, it was very good. And there was evening and there was morning, the sixth day.[1]

But by the second generation, that had changed. Adam and Eve's first-born son, Cain, was a farmer, and his brother, Abel, a shepherd—the first family's food was both red and green.

At some point, the brothers wanted to please the Lord with an offering. Each brought what he had: Cain offered grain, Abel offered meat. The Lord preferred the meat to the grain. No explanation is given for this preference, and no ground rules have been set prior to these primal offerings, revealing a universe that is troubling in its moral ambiguity—absurd, Cioran might say. In a jealous rage, Cain killed Abel.

Explanations abound in religious literature for the Lord's arbitrary bias and the resulting murder. Cain is a tiller of the soil, says the Talmud, while Abel is a caretaker of the flock. One takes, the other caretakes, and the Lord prefers the latter. The Qur'an concurs, stating that Abel made his offering out of duty while Cain made his selfishly. A modern-day evangelical apologist preaches to his readers: "I understand that you like doing things your own way. All of us do. It's natural. It goes way back to the days of Cain and Abel, when Cain tried to worship God his own way, while Abel did things God's way."[2]

Each of these justifications for the Lord's choice is made up out of thin air, fabricated by the imagination of the interpreter, but not emerging from the story itself.

The New Testament writers also want to explain this troubling text. In faith Abel offered to God a more acceptable sacrifice than Cain's, says the writer of Hebrews. First John adds, "We must not be like Cain who was from the evil one and murdered his brother. And why did he murder him? Because his own deeds were evil and his brother's righteous." Even Jesus refers to Abel as righteous, implying that Cain was not.

But Cain had no idea what constituted an acceptable sacrifice, and neither did Abel. Each gave what he had, and, without explanation, God liked the meat and disliked the grain.

At least one writer shoots straight. Rabbi Tanhuma bar Abba, around 400 CE, imagines these words in Cain's mouth after the Lord confronts him for killing his brother: "I killed him [because] you created in me the evil inclination. But You—You are the keeper of all things, why did you allow me to kill him? You are the one who killed him—You who are called I, for if you had accepted my sacrifice as you did his, I wouldn't have been jealous of him!"[3] According to the rabbi, the moral of the story is not a good one: God is responsible for Abel's death.

Regardless, humans got the message: God wants meat. The next meat sacrifice took place when Noah stepped off the ark, slaughtered one of each of the ritually-clean animals that he'd kept alive for months, and lit their flesh on fire. The odor of the sacrifice pleased the Lord, proclaims Torah, and blood sacrifice was off and running.

Christian theologian Stanley Hauerwas is fond of quoting his Jewish friend who said, "Any religion that doesn't tell you what to do with your pots and pans and genitals can't be interesting."[4] In other words, religions care about food and sex.

The Hebrews definitely cared about food. Twenty-six commandments (*mitzvoth*) govern food, and most of those are about eating animals. It's similar in Islam: meat is considered *halal* (lawful) only if it's butchered under specific conditions and using specific methods, all of which are meant to follow the Prophet Muhammed's command that slaughtered animals be treated as sentient beings and part of the community of creation.

My neighbor Dorjee told me that Tibetan Buddhists would rather kill a yak than a smaller animal because the meat-to-suffering ratio is better. Buddhism acknowledges that suffering is inevitable, a part of our existence. So the Buddhist precept is to reduce suffering as much as possible, which is why some Buddhists are vegetarians or vegans while others, like my neighbors, focus on eating meat from larger animals so that less death is required for each meal.

Religious people have been concerned about how to shed the blood of animals and eat their meat for thousands of years. Dietary laws are bound up in the founding myths—the founding murder—of the Abrahamic tradition. Our ancestors needed some theological cover for the messy business of killing and eating other creatures. My predecessors in the priesthood were among those doing the slaughtering, so clergy have had blood on our hands for millennia. The Roman haruspex stood before the emperor, disemboweled an animal, and told the augustus what the entrails portended. Hebrew priests slit the throats of oxen, and the blood poured down the altar into a catch basin (an ox has about 15 gallons of blood). Mayan shamans did the same.

By the time I entered seminary, animal sacrifice had been redacted from the clergy job description. We talked a lot about metaphorical blood, and we learned how to officiate the Eucharist, pretending that the grape juice in the thimble-sized plastic cups is like unto Jesus' blood. But in truth it's Welch's, bought in bulk at Costco, with King's Hawaiian bread standing in for Jesus' torn flesh.

When I was a pastor, one of my duties was to arrange the parade of petting-zoo animals down the aisles of the sanctuary on Christmas Eve—sheep, donkey, goat, and camel. I can attest that not one of them was slaughtered in front of the congregation. But imagine if we had. What was once the most commonplace of religious practices would have sent families in Christmas sweaters screaming for the exits. One of the most primal aspects of religion has been lost, to both the priests and the people.

To recover that, to get blood on my hands, I had to venture afield.

I walk under an arch topped with a bull skull, on my way to the barn behind the homestead we've rented for the week. Over my shoulders are slung two dozen pheasants, their cold weight pressing down on me. They hang from wire wickets attached to leather belts; their bodies roll off of one another and I struggle to balance them.

Some of the guys wanted to drop our birds at a lady's house who cleans them for $4.50 each—they've cleaned enough birds already on this trip, they say. I counter that if we're going to hunt, we really should clean our own birds. Someone suggests that we just breast them out. I offer to clean them all.

I struggle to find the light switch in the dark. Flipping it illuminates a couple of bare incandescent bulbs strung from the rafters. A piece of plywood propped between two sawhorses sags when I drop the mass of pheasants on it. A 30-gallon Rubbermaid garbage bin lined with a thick, 2-mil plastic bag holds the remnants of previous hunting parties: pheasant chaff and Coors Light cans.

A curious cat watches me from the hay loft and I hear bats flitting over my head. I know this'll take a couple of hours—maybe someone will bring me a beer and help me with a few of the birds. I flip open the blade on my knife. It says "Coastal Cutlery"—I got it from the shop of my brother's first ex-wife's dead grandfather, a lifetime ago. It's a great knife, both heavy and balanced in my hand, and it holds an edge through the tough work of butchery on a cold night.

I approach each bird the same, as Jorge taught me. First I peel away some feathers from the breast. Then, pinching up some skin, I cut a slit with the tip of the blade. Setting down the knife, I slide the index and middle fingers of each of my hands inside the skin and tear, separating skin from muscle, baring breasts. I keep pulling and peeling, exposing the entire front of the bird, navigating the skin up and over the thighs and knees until it catches on the tough top of the foot. Now I can start to smell pheasant, a unique odor that's strong but not unpleasant. I spread the bird's thighs until I hear and feel the snap of hip bones dislocating from sockets. I ease my knife into the muscle, cutting along the top of the thigh, up and around the hip ball, and out the other side. I set the separated legs aside.

Flipping the carcass over, I peel feathered skin off the pheasant's back. At the base of the neck, a thin membrane bulges like a balloon;

it's the bird's crop, a storage compartment for food. This one is full of corn. I pull up the collar of skin on the bird's neck, like rolling a turtleneck the wrong way. Having exposed the shoulders, I slice a V, cutting half-inch incisions on either side of the neck. Sometimes in a movie fight, one of the combatants will jab two fingers into a spot on his opponent where the base of neck meets the top of the chest, and the bad guy will drop immediately, incapacitated and clutching his throat. That's the very spot on the pheasant where I insert two fingers from each hand. Then, holding the bird over the garbage can, I tear it in two in a violent rending of flesh and bone. I hold in my left hand the breast and wings, in my right the head, back, and guts, which I drop into the garbage bin.

One bird down, many to go. It's cold out here, my fingers are red and raw. I nick my hand with the knife blade, but I can't feel it through the cold-numb. My blood mixes with the pheasants'—I refuse to wear latex gloves; I want to feel the bird's flesh on mine. Feathers and viscous liquids stick to everything—my hands, the knife, my clothes. One after the other, the birds pile up on the table. I settle into it, the monotony, the rhythm, the routine.

Years ago, at the height of my ministry, I visited the headquarters of the worldwide leader in "protein solutions" in Arkansas. Over the course of a day, I met the billionaire grandson of the founder, a bunch of middle managers in an office building, and the minimum wage workers at a chicken kill plant. The middle managers wore khakis and Under Armour golf shirts and attended First Baptist with Pastor Ronnie Floyd and belonged to country clubs and lived in McMansions in the suburbs. They golfed and talked about college football. I was there with a group on a multi-million dollar grant. The middle managers seemed to dislike us, and the feeling was mutual. They saw us as elitist liberals, there to observe Middle America like visiting a zoo. We saw them as evidence of what's wrong with America.

My experience at the factory, however, was the opposite.

Trucks full of 28-day-old chickens lined up for a mile outside the plant. One by one they dumped their loads into a room lit by black lights to keep the birds calm, where immigrants from the Marshall Islands grabbed them rapid-fire and hung them upside down in metal stirrups at the beginning of a serpentine conveyor system. At the rate of 35-per-minute, the chickens' heads were dragged through a small pool of electrified water, stunning them just long enough for a whirring razorblade to slit their throats. As the conveyor moved the birds out into the massive factory, blood drained from their bodies into a trough in the floor. (That drains to holding tanks outside, we were told, and gets turned into lipstick.) The rest of the process is pretty straightforward: chickens gutted, de-feathered, washed, entombed in plastic, boxed, stacked on pallets.

A couple of the factory workers were granted special dispensation by their supervisor to leave their spots on the floor and join us in the break room, where we drank bad coffee out of styrofoam cups. We sat at a conference table. The workers stood and declined our offers to sit, amplifying the differences between us. We wore khakis and blazers, they wore hairnets and aprons smeared with blood.

I remember one woman in particular. Thin and white, she looked about 60 to me, but she was probably 10 years younger than that. She leaned on the door jamb, looking down into her coffee. She told us that she'd worked at the plant for 20 years; it had changed a lot—it used to be all white people, but now lots of immigrants, Karen and Marshallese; she didn't mind; they're good people, they work hard; this is a good place to work, they treat us good; the people who work in the plant are like a family; we celebrate birthdays and anniversaries together, and we all know about each other's kids; one of my daughters works in the plant, too, so I get to see her every day.

That woman has never left me; maybe I'm romanticizing her and her labor. With the exception of the sunfish that my mom filleted on the dock, neither of my parents ever killed an animal and prepped it for consumption. In the Joneses and the Hawthornes, knowledge of slaughter and butchery that went back untold generations and tens of thousands of years came to a screeching halt sometime in the 1930s when Ralph took a job at a tire store, Florence went to work for a bank, Bower started at the Minneapolis *Tribune*, and Jane went to college. My grandparents reared my parents in town, not on a farm, then sent them to college, all so that they wouldn't have to butcher animals. My parents settled in the suburbs and reared me in a rambler, drove me to

Cub Scouts and basketball, helped me get a good SAT score. An upgrade, it would seem, from our forebears who had to work the soil and slaughter animals to survive.

But that civilized world abandoned me mid-life, and I longed for something primal, something that could connect me to my ancestors. I often think of that woman, clearly uncomfortable among us and anxious to escape the conference room and get back to the killing floor. Over two decades, she'd prepped tens of thousands of chickens for American consumers. She'd fed me. She knows butchery and death, she's not reviled by blood and guts. She was a lot more like my ancestors than I was. I could translate Greek and Hebrew, preach entertaining sermons and debate arcane theological minutiae. But I lived in a rambler in the suburbs, golfed occasionally, and attended a megachurch with people just like me. What I didn't like about the middle managers was what I didn't like about myself—we'd all lost touch with something our ancestors knew well, we'd outsourced the butchery of our meat, insulated ourselves from the blood and muscle and sinew of the animals we eat.

So these days I'm happy to butcher all the birds.

I've stacked them up, denuded of feather and skin and bowels, a slippery pyramid of pheasant meat. A garden hose with a sprayer screwed on the end hangs from a thick nail on the wall. I retrieve it. The hose, stiff from the cold, reluctantly snakes behind me as I pull it to the table. Water spits and chokes out at first, and then flows in a steady stream, and I adjust the pattern to midway between jet and cone. All the birds are piled on one side of the table. I spray guts and blood and feathers off the other side. Then I hose down each carcass and transfer it to the clean side of the table. The water is cold. My hands, now even more numb, move in slow motion. I have to think to make my fingers work.

The last step is to bag up the birds. Larry gave me a box of the cheapest zip-top bags he could find at the Platte grocery story, Family Brand or something like that. I pull off the zippered cardboard tab at the top and yank out a bag. Everything's wet—my hands, the birds, the table, the bags. To be legal for transport, each carcass must have at least a foot and a feathered wing attached to prove they're roosters. I cup a wing around the meaty breast and drop it in a bag, followed by two legs. The thump in the bag is satisfying; the zip of the bag is satisfying; watching the assortment of meat pile up in the cooler is satisfying. The weight of the cooler full of meat is satisfying.

This is what I've needed, this simple satisfaction. The feel of the knife cutting through muscle, the snap of bone in my hand. As I limp the cooler back to the truck, hefting it on my right leg with each step, I consider, as I did with the venison, what I'll do with the meat. A lot of it will go into pheasant sausage, ground with pork fatback, fennel seeds, garlic, lemon rind, and Madeira wine, then piped into casings and hung in the garage—my family's favorite pheasant fare. Some I'll pound flat, dredge through milk and egg and breadcrumbs, and fry in a bath of butter. Some will go on the smoker, absorbing cherry and apple wood fumes. All of it I will serve and eat it with a sense of fulfillment and with gratitude.

Anyone who butchers another animal finds their own creatureliness right in the crosshairs. Like the rooster and the doe, I'm made up of muscle and bone, innards and hide.

A century before I studied theology to its terminus, a Lutheran named Rudolf Otto pursued the same course and, after a life-changing trip around the world in 1910–1911 during which he observed many different religious ceremonies, he wrote one of the classic theological texts of the twentieth century, *The Idea of the Holy*. Like all theologians of his generation, Otto was indebted to the work of the godfather of modern theology, Friedrich Schleiermacher. Prior to Schleiermacher, Immanuel Kant had argued that human experiences are structured in our minds by the existing categories that we bring to each experience. Schleiermacher countered Kant, arguing that religious experience is something different, unique. In the eighteenth century, religion came under a withering assault from science and the Enlightenment, the beginning of the denouement of organized religion that we're living through today. Schleiermacher wanted to rescue religion by telling its critics that they were closer to the true spirit of religion than the reified rites and dogmas of the church. "The contemplation of the pious," he wrote, "is the *immediate consciousness* of the universal existence of all finite things, in and through the Infinite, and of all temporal things in and through the Eternal."[5] We arrive at that consciousness of God when we experience the *feeling of utter dependence*, which is the "highest grade of immediate self-consciousness," and an "essential element of human nature."[6] In other words, when we feel lost and alone, overwhelmed and small, that's when we experience God; when we realize that we're dependent, we're de facto acknowledging that there's something bigger than us. That something is God.

A hundred years after Schleiermacher, Otto put a finer point on it. What we're actually experiencing when we feel utterly dependent, Otto says, is our own *creatureliness*—he calls it *creature-feeling* or *creature-consciousness*, "the emotion of a creature, submerged and overwhelmed by its own nothingness in contrast to that which is supreme above all creatures."[7] During a genuine religious event, we experience the *mysterium tremendum et fascinans*—the mystery, both terrifying and fascinating. Some might call it a "delightful Horrour."

The mystery is frightening and alluring; the mystery is our experience of God, catalyzed by our experience of our own creatureliness.

That's what happened to me in Doug's duck boat. Cold and wet and lost, I was terrified *and* euphoric. I acutely experienced my smallness relative to the massive lake, the miles of wilderness that surrounded us, the untamable storm. And when it was over, I could not wait to go back.

I saw it in my kids' faces when we arrived at the dock, having survived our trek across Gunflint Lake in a gale. They were electric. Same with the guys when we rafted the Gorge.

While deer hunting, I feel it again. The killing is simultaneously abhorrent and alluring. As I pull the trigger, my body pulses with excitement. But I watch the doe struggle, fall, and flail on the forest floor, kicking her legs as the life drains from her—the life that I have taken from her. Grief pierces me, enough that I consider vowing never to shoot another deer. Similarly ambivalent feelings course through me as I gut her. And then, at the butchering, fascination eclipses terror.

Over the course of a day, I've ridden the sine wave of *mysterium tremendum et fascinans* with this deer. It's brought into sharp relief my own creatureliness, and it's also put me in contact with something holy. Otto, noting the moral and ethical connotations in the word "holy," coined a new term to describe this experience: the *numinous*. From the Latin *numen*, which means divinity, divine presence, or divine will, Otto describes the numinous almost poetically:

> The feeling of it may at times come sweeping like a gentle tide pervading the mind with a tranquil mood of deepest worship. It may pass over into a more set and lasting attitude of the soul, continuing, as it were, thrillingly vibrant and resonant. . . . It may burst in sudden eruption up from the depths of the soul with spasms and convulsions, or lead to the strangest excitements, to intoxicated frenzy, to transport, and to ecstasy . . . it may be developed into something beautiful and pure and glorious. It may become the hushed, trembling, and speechless humility of the creature in the presence of—whom or what? In the presence of that which is a *mystery* inexpressible and above all creatures.[8]

I've never run across a theological concept that better describes my experience in wild places than the numinous. I venture to wild places to put my own creatureliness front-and-center in my consciousness, and to experience the numinous—that which is beyond me, greater than me.

And nothing brings my creatureliness into focus like killing, butchering, and consuming another creature.

On the last day of the last pheasant hunt of the year, we hit a parcel of land that Larry owns, about 20 miles north of Huron. This spot is gorgeous, with four large food plots, a cattail slough, and a creek twisting through it—I once had a dream about heaven, and it took place on this farm. Birds pop from various spots as we try to surround them or push them or block them. A tailless rooster takes flight from snow-covered cattails, and I hesitate for a moment but still manage to bring him down.

One guy after another peels off from the group, headed for home, leaving only Jorge and me to make one last push from south to north toward our trucks. We abandon our plan to walk the food plots, and instead follow the brook. I walk on the frozen creek bed while Jorge hikes the high bank. Albert crisscrosses in front of me, Crosby on his heel. Both banks boast bunches of vegetation. The dogs stick their noses in each. Out flies a rooster to my left, attempting to gain altitude over the riverbank. I fire and he drops in the field beyond. The dogs bust through the crusty snowbank and come back with the bird.

Back at the trucks, Jorge and I split up the day's take, shake hands, and bid one another farewell.

"I'll see you next year," he calls to me as I climb in the truck. "Unless the cancer gets me first!"

The sky is fading gray to black as I pull off the gravel road and onto pavement. North to Redfield, about 20 miles, and then east on Highway 212 all the way home. Through eastern South Dakota and southwestern Minnesota, the speed limit drops from 55 to 30 every few miles as I roll through towns named Frankfort, Doland, Clark, Henry, Kampeska, Watertown, Kranzburg, Dawson, Montevideo, Granite Falls, Sacred Heart, Renville, Danube, Olivia, Bird Island, Stewart, Brownton, Glencoe, Plato, Norwood Young America, Cologne. Each twinkles with Christmas bulbs. Plastic garlands in the shapes of stars, stockings, and snowflakes hang from lampposts. Spotlighted nativity scenes share space in the cities' public parks with World War II cannons. MERRY CHRISTMAS is spelled in lights, strung across Main Streets.

My phone rings. It's Jorge. I answer it on speaker in the truck. He wants to know how the drive is going, how the roads are. He tells me that he and Connie just ate a pheasant for dinner, one that we killed today. There's joy in his voice—joy at being alive, joy at memories of the hunt, joy at gaining strength by taking the pheasant's body into his own body.

Like the vast majority of human beings, Jorge and I are carnivores. And like so many of our ancestors, we are intimately involved in the acquisition of the meat that we eat. That's reason enough for joy.

9

Death

The secret cause of all suffering is mortality itself, which is the prime condition of life. It cannot be denied if life is to be affirmed.

—Joseph Campbell, *The Power of Myth*

I DON'T REMEMBER WHEN I FIRST KILLED AN ANIMAL WITH MY hands. But I do remember the first one I killed in front of my children. On a drizzly October day, I'd pitched a ground blind near the edge of a lake, overlooking a crease in the water between reeds and lily pads. My kids were young at the time, probably 10, 9, and 6. None had hunted, and only one—Tanner, a Cub Scout—had shot a firearm, and just a .22 at that. The kids sat, bored and fidgety, hoping to see dad shoot a duck and Albert retrieve it.

A ground blind is not ideal for duck hunting. Basically a small camouflage tent, its window cut-outs don't allow a shooter to swing a shotgun, making it better suited for hunting something that doesn't fly, like deer or turkey; I'd chosen it to hide my kids' movements from the ducks. I hoped that a bird would land in the sliver of water that I could see, and that's exactly what happened. I shot a small, green-winged teal about a foot off the water.

Albert blasted from the blind, hit the water, and swam to the duck, which was still alive. Sometimes birds are dead in the water, and some will die in the dog's mouth en route back to the handler. But oftentimes, the dog delivers a live bird. This duck was still very much alive when Albert dropped her in the grass at our feet. She sat up and looked around. She tried to walk and failed—shotgun pellets had broken her leg and her wing, injuries that prohibited her escape mechanisms—flying, swimming, and running—but otherwise not diminishing her life-force.

I reached down with my left hand and gently but forcefully pushed down on her back with the meaty part of my palm. Then, with my dominant right hand I grasped her head and twisted. Sinews popped in her neck, legs kicked, wings flapped. I released the twist, but she kept kicking and flapping. I twisted again. More kicking and flapping.

I twisted again and her head came off in my hand. I dropped her body and, like the proverbial chicken, she tried to run around. I've since read that although her spinal neural network kept firing for a few seconds, telling her body to perform familiar functions like running and flying, I'd separated her body from her somatosensory cortex, which sends nerve signals to the brain. In other words, she was feeling no pain, which brings me some comfort.

My children, however, were horrified. They'd climbed out of bed to join dad on a fun little hunt, and they'd instead witnessed a violent act that left my hands dripping with blood and a headless bird flapping at their feet. What I'd done was humane but also barbaric, primitive, and brutal.

We sat for a while more, but the kids couldn't take their eyes off of the decapitated teal. And, obeying his 300 million olfactory receptors, Albert kept sniffing and licking and generally messing with her carcass. No more ducks landed in the lake, and we called it quits. I threw her head into the woods and carried her body by a leg back to the cabin for cleaning.

That bit of savagery took place early in my pursuit of hunting. Since then, I have killed hundreds of animals, some of them with my hands.

Death stalks hunting. Not just death, but dying.

I sit in a deer stand, listening for the sound of footfall on leaves, my teeth clattering. Three whitetail does emerge. Slowly, quietly, I reach for my rifle, keeping my eye on the largest of the three. Slowly, slowly, I shoulder the gun.

In the scope, I see nothing but darkness. Then a crescent of grass, a tree trunk, and it again goes black. I'm not looking straight down the scope—I'm cockeyed. I breathe through my nose, calm myself, rest my cheek on the cold stock.

There we go, now I can see through the scope. But where are the deer? I pull my head back a bit, look over the scope, locate the deer on the move, adjust the rifle in their direction and lower my eye back to the scope. I switch off the safety, and that unnatural, metallic note stops the does in their tracks. In the silent November woods, that ting doesn't belong, and they know it. The doe at whom I've taken aim looks directly at me, or so it seems. But she doesn't see me. I'm 15 feet above the ground in a ladder stand, the equivalent of an adult highchair, lashed with nylon straps to an ash tree. Although the occasional bobcat will jump from a tree branch and take out a young fawn, this doe's predators—wolves and coyotes and automobiles—come at her from ground level. Nothing in her experience tells her to look up, so she looks under me, past me, her ears searching for another out-of-place sound.

Through the scope I can see her fur, brown with flecks of white. I move the crosshairs to the pleat behind her front shoulder. I insert my finger into the trigger guard, feel for the trigger, exhale, and squeeze. The loud crack, muffled by my earplugs, echoes through the trees, and the deer scatter. My heart is pounding. I start breathing again.

Doubt pours over me. Did I hit her? Was it a kill shot?

A couple years ago, my brother, Andrew, was hunting elk in Eastern Oregon. He sunk a bullet into a large bull, but it sauntered away. He tracked it and found it on its knees, still alive. At close range, he put another bullet into the beast. The elk looked at him and snorted. Another bullet. Still alive. Out of bullets, he panicked and wondered how to kill the elk, looking for a stick or a rock, reduced to the tools of the earliest hunters. Ultimately, the elk died of blood loss from the bullet wounds. You'd think my brother would have anticipated this, being that he's a surgeon and well-acquainted with the damage inflicted by gunshots. But faced with a wounded animal five times his size looking him in the eye, he lost his composure and his good sense.

I unload my rifle and tie it to a rope that hangs from the tree stand and lower it to the ground. Then I lift the safety bar, like a skier preparing to get off a chairlift, and descend the steel rungs. I have to remove my gloves to untie the knot around the gun; my hands are shaking.

As I walk in the direction that the doe fled, I examine the ground. The sky is dirty dishwater gray, the light flat and shadowless. I'm searching for a crimson drop of blood amidst the polychrome sea of debris on the forest floor.

There's one. And another.

And there she is, lying on her side, awkwardly jammed between two trees. Her eyes see me and her front legs kick. I've hit her two inches high, missing the quick kill of a double-lung shot. Instead, I severed her spine. She's going to die. Eventually. The question before me is whether to hasten her quietus with another shot. And the subsequent question is where to place that shot, in the body or the head.

Shooting a large mammal at 50 or 100 or 150 yards, eyed through a scope, requires no great fortitude. But standing an arm's length away and shooting her in the head—well, that's another matter.

Let her die slowly, I think. Maybe that's what I should do. Should I stay here with her, or walk away and let her die without the fear invoked by her predator standing over her?

She is definitely afraid. I can see it in her eyes.

When my dad first went to the ER, we sent him against his wishes.

On a Wednesday morning, my mom called and told me that he'd fallen out of bed during the night, and she couldn't get him up.

He was heavy, about 265 pounds. When he'd retired a decade earlier, I bet he weighed 210, and 10 years before that, 180.

Retirement didn't suit my dad, though he'd long anticipated it. He and his partners sold their business in 2004 and pocketed a tidy sum. Dad told us that the first thing he would do with the money was buy himself a new car. He constantly researched vehicles in *Consumer Reports* in search of the best one. When he died in 2018, he was still driving the same 1999 Acura. He was a deliberator; answers eluded him. He also spent hundreds of hours in those retirement years playing the solitaire game that came pre-installed on his Windows PC. He drank coffee till noon, ate Burger King for lunch, and started pouring Jack Daniels over rocks when the nightly news came on at 5:30.

After the call from my mom, I drove the two blocks to their house. In the unlikely pose of a Roman emperor at banquet, Dad lay on the floor, propped up on one elbow. He told me that he'd needed to use the bathroom in the middle of the night. His legs had given way when he tried to get out of bed, and he collapsed to the floor.

I asked him when it happened, how long he'd been on the floor. He didn't know. He said that if I could just help him up, he'd be fine. My mom and I maneuvered him to a sitting position. He asked for his walker, thinking that he could pull himself up. He couldn't. We abandoned the walker. I stepped around behind him, crouched, put my hands in his armpits, and lifted. That didn't work either. My mom asked if my bad back can handle this. I didn't reply.

My dad wasn't a hugger, at least not of me. Straight from central casting of a Lake Wobegon monologue, he grew up in a small town and embodied Max Weber's Protestant: work hard, save a lot, don't have much fun, and feel bad about yourself. Showing emotion, hugging, those kinds of things were frowned upon.

I circled him, straddling his legs, his pajamas akimbo and falling off. As I squatted down it occurred to me that he had needed to use the bathroom—how many hours ago was that? Is he wearing his diapers? Both his front diaper and his back diaper? I couldn't summon the nerve to ask him. My mom told me to lift with my legs. Face-to-face with my dad, I put my arms under his armpits and tried to clasp my fingers behind him. I couldn't. Instead, I leaned into his chest and, using the bed frame behind him as counter pressure, jimmied him up. He wrapped his arms around me, hug-like.

He looked at me with big eyes and said that he needed to go to the bathroom. Now!

Until that moment, the worst thing I'd ever smelled was the time that my basement freezer conked out while I was on vacation in August and about 30 pheasants turned into maggot nests. That odor was suddenly relegated to second place.

My eyes watered and I thought, he must have shit himself (a fact later confirmed by my mother). I gagged.

Faced with delivering my father to the toilet and our joint humiliation, I instead fled. I reached out and grabbed his walker, put it in front of him, set his hands on the handles, and left the room.

He got to the toilet, my mom told me a few minutes later in the front hallway. She said that I should go to work, which I did. Then, as I sat in a meeting, my phone started buzzing. I excused myself to go to the bathroom and, standing at the urinal, listened to the successive voicemails: your dad couldn't get up from the toilet, and I couldn't get him up. He told me not to call the paramedics, but I did. They're on the way. They're taking him to the ER. He doesn't want to go, but they say he has to. When can you get there?

Two weeks after that, it happens again, on a Wednesday.

On Ash Wednesday.

My mom calls and asks me to come over. She'd been at a doctor's appointment with her friend, Shirley. When they left, dad was sitting on a bench getting dressed; when they returned, he was on his hands and knees on the bedroom floor, trying to make it to the bed. She'd been gone four hours.

When I arrive, he's kneeling next to the bed, with his elbows on the mattress and his hands clasped. I see a bloody knot on his forehead.

I ask how he hit his head. He doesn't know.

I wrestle him onto the bed using the same tactic as last time, a move I've now mastered.

Shirley says we should call an ambulance since he's on blood thinners.

My mom calls Andrew.

Andrew says call an ambulance.

Dad struggles to speak, his words aphasically jumbled. His face morphs from calm to confused, though not angry, when the stroke-like syntax emerges from his mouth.

The ambulance arrives and two paramedics enter the bedroom. I remember one of them, named Dominic, from my years as a police chaplain. He bears a smear of black ash on his forehead. When I was a pastor, the imposition of ashes was the most intimate moment of the year. When I served communion, people tended to look down at the bread changing hands during the quick interaction. But on Ash Wednesday, they looked me right in the eye. And I touched their foreheads—an act of intimacy, to touch another person's face. I'd rub my right thumb in the greasy mix of oil and ash from last year's burnt palm branches and smear them on the teenager, feeling the bumps of his pimples beneath my thumb. I'd push aside the woman's bangs and notice how much makeup she's wearing. I'd reach up for the forehead of the man I know is cheating on his wife. Flecks of ash floated down onto their noses. Some people cried. I told them that from dust they came and to dust they shall return—basically, I reminded them that they are going to die.

Dominic straps my father to a gurney and rolls him out of the house for the last time. I drive to the hospital and receive my blaze orange VISITOR sticker and the person at the desk buzzes me through the doors to the ER. Same room as last time. Same doctors and nurses.

They rush me out of the room when he starts having a bowel movement in his bed.

Looking at his large, white belly, a nurse says, "I see we have a touch of ringworm."

Two neurologists hold up cards and ask him to say what he sees. He struggles to speak. Hammock. Cactus. Glove. Chair.

Then this interaction.

NURSE (NEARLY SHOUTING): Douglas, we need to know if you want us to revive you.

DAD: What?

NURSE: If you stop breathing, do you want us to put a tube down your throat?

ME: We have his DNR on file at the hospital already.

NURSE: But if he is conscious, then his own wishes override the DNR. We need to ask him these questions. Douglas, if you stop breathing, do you want us to put a tube down your throat?

ME: Dad, do you want to be intubated? You don't want to be intubated, do you? That's what you wrote in your health care directive.

DAD: What?

NURSE: Douglas, if you stop breathing, do you want us to put a tube down your throat to help you breathe?

DAD: Tony, what should I say? I don't know what to say.

NURSE: Douglas, if your heart stops, do you want us to perform
chest compressions?

DAD: Tony, what should I say?

ME: Dad, tell them to follow the health care directive.

NURSE: Douglas, do you want us to perform chest compressions if
your heart stops beating?

DAD: I don't know what to say. Tony, what should I say?

I look at my father's face, trying to discern his state of mind, trying
to understand what he wants. He is afraid, I can see it in his eyes.

He does not know that he is dying.

He dies two days later, the third day of Lent.

Some people euthanize their own dogs—years ago I found the body of
a yellow Lab with a bullet hole in its head in a ditch on our property—
but I am not able to.

Nor am I able to shoot this deer in the head. Instead, standing
about 10 yards away, I take aim at the spot where my first shot should
have hit, and I fire. Both her lungs quickly fill with blood, and she dies
before my eyes.

The first deer I ever shot never quartered toward me, so she never
exposed the so-called "bread basket" for which deer hunters aim. I only
had a straight-on shot, so that's the shot I took. She had crossed a
stream from a part of our land that is, for all intents and purposes, an
island, bound by a creek on one side and the lake on the other. Deer
prefer to cross that creek only on our driveway, under which the creek
runs through a culvert, or at another point further south where the
creek is narrow and shallow, a spot we call the Funnel. After deer si-
phon through the creek, they come into a willow thicket, in which they
can hide and get their bearings with some shelter from predators.

The willow thicket, however, affords no protection from a bullet.

I fired into her chest and she bounded out of the thicket, inexpli-
cably toward me. She pinballed off of one tree, then another, and then
collapsed in the maple leaves beneath my tree stand.

I descended and walked over to her. I was 49 years old, and she was the first mammal I'd killed on a hunt. Her eyes, lately luminous, were open, and her tongue hung out the side of her mouth, two characteristics that I've seen on every dead deer I've witnessed since and that I wish were not a part of the ritual. If her eyes had been closed, it would have been easier.

I don't want to die. I share that instinct with all fauna. Deer flee wolves; I stop at red lights. A panicked doe with a severed spinal cord doesn't want to die. Neither does a duck with a broken wing or an injured pheasant—I've had them claw at me from inside the game pouch of my hunting vest, not quite dead. A couple years ago, a pheasant whose neck I'd wrung jumped out of my vest and escaped. He wasn't ready to die.

My dad didn't want to die. In spite of our conversations about health care directives and DNRs, when the time came, he was not ready.

The ancient Stoics advise us to be ready at all times. In the first century CE, Seneca wrote,

> Death is on my trail, and life is fleeting away; teach me something with which to face these troubles. Bring it to pass that I shall cease trying to escape from death, and that life may cease to escape from me. Give me courage to meet hardships; make me calm in the face of the unavoidable. Relax the straitened limits of the time which is allotted me. Show me that the good in life does not depend upon life's length, but upon the use we make of it.[1]

What cripples us in life is not the inevitability of death, the Stoics preached, but the fear of death. By rehearsing our own deaths daily, we purge ourselves of that fear. And keeping death always before us prompts us to live better lives, to live each day as if it's our last. In old still-life paintings, next to a vase of flowers and some pottery on a shelf, the skull is a reminder to *memento mori*, remember that you're going to die.

Wild places are full of *memento mori* moments, killing an animal with luminous brown eyes chief among them. Hunting puts my own death right before me. I know it's coming, I admit that it's inevitable. I read the obituaries in the newspaper and notice how many people in there are, like me, in their fifties. He died suddenly and unexpectedly or after a long battle with depression or surrounded by family and we'd especially like to thank the hospice staff who made his final days so comfortable. She had a great career and volunteered at church, but she loved her grandchildren most of all. On his 50th birthday he parachuted out of an airplane, which had long been on his bucket list. She didn't want a funeral but instead asked for a party, so we're asking everyone to wear tie-dye shirts. Instead of flowers, please send a donation in his name to the charity of your choice.

They're tucked back there every day, in tiny print in the back of the Metro section, paid for by the column-inch, all of our dead. And on Wednesdays in the fall, on the back page of the Sports section, are color photos of hunters clad in orange, kneeling by dead deer, grasping antlers and smiling—grip-n-grins, they're called. Deer with their eyes open and tongues out. Then on Thursdays come the letters to the editor, complaining about the savagery of these photos. Haven't we evolved beyond this primitive tradition of killing and eating animals? The newspaper should not be glorifying this butchery. What did the deer ever do to you?

We've sequestered death, pushed it off to arm's length. We leave it to the ambulance drivers and doctors and nurses and morticians. Hunting has changed that for me in a way that religion never did. Deciding with my brothers and mother to remove life support and let my father die was not like ringing the neck of a duck or firing a bullet through the lungs of a whitetail deer. But it wasn't totally unlike it, either.

Because as well as reflecting on the inevitability of my own death, I've made the conscious choice to cause death. Anyone who eats meat causes death, but it's usually outsourced to people who work at kill plants. I've chosen to actively participate in the death of my fellow creatures, to end their lives and to take their flesh into my body as food.

They were going to die anyway. Not a single pheasant, duck, goose, grouse, or deer that I've shot was immortal. Had I not killed them, each would have died, most of them violently—very few prey animals die of old age. And predators like me are also destined to die. Hunting is my rehearsal for my own death, my obedience to the inscription over the door at St. Paul's Monastery on Mt. Athos: "If you die before you die, you won't die when you die."

My ancestors who hunted to survive were familiar with death, and I can't help but think that they feared their own death less as a result. I want to fear my own death less, so I hunt.

I dug my robe out of the back of the closet. My family asked me to preach the homily at Dad's funeral. I stood up in the pulpit, talking about him, and thinking about how much he loved seeing me preach, and about how long it had been since I'd been up there.

We buried Dad's ashes on the same island of land where deer hide during hunting season. I ordered a granite tombstone from the chain-smoking proprietor of Cuyuna Monument Company in Crosby, Minnesota. I swung through his U-shaped driveway as instructed, and he and I lifted the stone into my truck. Back at the cabin, we transferred it to the UTV and drove Mom on a trail to the spot she'd picked out. We put a bench out there, too. And a bottle of Jack Daniels, from which I take a slug whenever I visit his grave.

Mom says she's going to plant wildflowers around the tombstone this summer, but I don't think they'll grow that deep in the woods.

10

God

I know plenty of people who find God most reliably in books, in buildings, and even in other people. I have found God in all of these places too, but the most reliable meeting place for me has always been creation. . . . Where other people see acreage, timber, soil, and river frontage, I see God's body, or at least as much of it as I am able to see. In the only wisdom I have at my disposal, the Creator does not live apart from creation but spans and suffuses it. When I take a breath, God's Holy Spirit enters me. When a cricket speaks to me, I talk back. Like everything else on earth, I am an embodied soul, who leaps to life when I recognize my kin. If this makes me a pagan, then I am a grateful one.

—Barbara Brown Taylor, *Leaving Church*

PAUL, THE RECIPIENT OF MY SEVENTH-GRADE DECLARATION OF intent to be a minister, took me to the Boundary Waters for the first time. I was 14, as were the half-dozen other kids on the trip. We unloaded the church van, Paul chugged an entire glass bottle of Pepto Bismol, and we pushed off in tank-like Alumacraft canoes.

After the better part of a week, we sat around the campfire on our final night in the wilderness. One of us asked Paul why he hadn't led us in a Bible study or even a prayer—this was a church trip, after all.

Firelight dancing across his face, Paul swept his arms across the lake beside us, raised his palms to the starry sky, and said, "How could you be out here in God's creation and not be in a constant state of prayer?"

That one-sentence sermon was so powerful that I remember it verbatim, four decades later. He'd chosen not to preach to us that week, not to draw analogies between the waters we paddled and the waters of baptism, not to pull out his Bible and school us on Jesus and the prophets. Instead he trusted us to find God in the wilderness. The forest was our teacher, the lakes our Bible, the fire our prayer.

I've navigated a similar tack heretofore, avoiding didactic lessons on the divine, possibly leaving readers frustrated that I've not talked more pointedly about the God of the title.

My motives are less noble than Paul's were. Years ago, after reading the court-ordered psychological evaluation that brought a hot knot to the base of my throat, I asked my therapist, "Am I a narcissist?"

"Let's put it this way," she said. "I don't get up in the morning and think, *I'm going to climb into a pulpit and tell people about God.*"

From age 15 to age 40, I did just that, making a pretty good living at telling people what to think about God. I climbed a ladder, but not St. John Climacus's ladder of divine ascent. It was the demon Narcissus's ladder of professional ascent: from Sunday school teacher and church camp counselor to globetrotting preacher and author. It was the wrong ladder, and I fell off.

Grandpa Ralph used to joke: it's not the fall that gets you, it's the sudden stop at the end. The wind that got knocked out of me at the bottom of my fall included my confidence for proclaiming definitive words about an ineffable Mystery. My current reluctance to tell people how to think about God is hard-earned, and I beg the reader's forgiveness. I will try to remedy that deficiency in the pages that remain, albeit gingerly.

The faith in which I was raised was radically dualistic, drawing a bright line between spirit and matter, body and soul, human and God. God is Wholly Other, I was taught, not just unlike me in every way, but unlike everything in every way. "Who is like the Lord our God?" the psalmist asks rhetorically. The answer is so obvious that it does not even need to be stated: no one, and no thing. God is pure spirit, alone at the top of the chain. Although the wholly immaterial God is mediated to us through material objects—the Bible; a nibble of bread and a sip of grape juice—material stuff is generally thought of as bad. The goal of life is, upon death, to slough off the material and join God in a purely spiritual afterlife—promises of "resurrection bodies" notwithstanding. That's what we were taught, more a legacy of Plato than of Jesus. The tentacles of dualism are insidious, snaking themselves into all sorts of unexpected places. Again, consider prayer. Dualistic Christianity posits that the wholly other, purely spiritual God occasionally breaks into our material reality and makes stuff happen, sticking a finger into the cocktail of creation and swizzling. This activity of God is often predicated on my behavior: if I pray hard enough, or with the right formula, or with a righteous heart, then God will enter the space-time continuum and do what I ask. This recipe, prevalent in most religions, reverses our roles, turning God into a puppet and me into a marionette.

Or consider salvation. On my ordination day, still aglow from the experience, I poked my head in the office of the senior pastor, my boss. He complimented me on my ordination paper and oral defense. But, he said, I got one thing wrong: when I explicated the *ordo salutis* (order of salvation), I implied that we cooperate with God on the final step, our sanctification. "We don't have anything to do with our own salvation," he corrected me. "It's 100 percent God, and zero percent us." He was channeling his favorite theologian, Karl Barth, who wrote, "The power of God can be detected neither in the world of nature nor in the souls of men."[1] That's dualism: a bright line between God and us.

Dualism is also at least partly to blame for the damage that we've caused to the environment. When a theology subordinates the physical to the spiritual, it degrades all materiality in the eyes of its adherents: why should we care about any of this material when the immaterial is so much more important?

But I've come to believe that the line between the material and the immaterial isn't so bright. Take this example from what philosophers call the "extended mind thesis": Inga has heard about a museum exhibit, and she makes plans to go. She remembers where the museum is, and she starts walking there. Otto has also heard about the exhibit, and he'd also like to see it. But he can't remember where the museum is, because Otto has Alzheimer's. However, Otto always carries a notebook with him, and he's assiduous about recording any information that he thinks he'll need later. Upon hearing about the exhibit, Otto opens his notebook, flips through pages until he sees the name and address of the museum, and uses that information to walk to the museum and see the exhibit.[2]

Otto uses his notebook in the same way that Inga uses her brain—the notebook is part of Otto's memory, an extension of his mind. Otto undermines dualism. These tools that we use are extensions of us—in some way, they are part of us. The difference between Otto's brain and his notebook is clear. But between his *mind* and his notebook? Not so clear.

What I'm calling *mind*, Plato and Aristotle called *nous*—the intellectual awareness that constitutes human ontological uniqueness in creation. Others call it *spirit* or *soul*. But unlike the ancients, I'm not suggesting that my mind is some immaterial essence of me that's trapped inside the prison of my flesh. On the contrary, my mind is very much physical, housed inside my skull. But it doesn't end there. My mind extends beyond my body. I'm more than my body, though my body is inextricable from what constitutes me.[3] The boundaries between body and soul, brain and mind, material and spiritual aren't so clear. In fact, they may not exist at all. I'm a mix of physical and spiritual, material and immaterial, two elements that, when mixed, create a new compound.

It's the same with God. However God exists spiritually, that existence extends into the physical world. Material reality—that is, creation—is God's notebook, an extension of God. And just as Otto's notebook tells us something about Otto, God's notebook reveals to us something about God.

Theologians call this *natural theology*: the idea that God can be found without the aid of miracles, scripture, or any source from outside the material realm. By looking at the way things are here, in the real world, we can deduce a lot about the Creative Force that's behind the world.

I've used natural theology a bit differently herein, not to prove the existence of God, but instead to investigate the Numinous. I've tried to obey my youth pastor's lakeside injunction: I've tried to pay attention, especially in wild places, to the signs and rhythms that indicate transcendence, that point me to the divine, that help me read God's notebook.

I've learned:

The God of wild places offers peace. In a modern world that's frenetic and busy—always connected, always *on*—finding peace is getting more difficult. Meditation apps promise to cure this ailment, but it's a tragic irony that we're looking for a remedy from a device that's done more to eliminate peace than any tool we've ever invented. To receive the peace offered by the God of wild places, we'll have to retrograde to old technologies: canoe and paddle; hiking boots and walking stick; bow and arrow and fishing pole. We also have to remember that the peace we long for is within, a spark of the divine that resides within each of us. To bring that spark to a flame can be done indoors, but I have a lot more luck when I'm outdoors—and the wilder the place the better.

The God of wild places honors place. When we visit and revisit the wild places that are special to us, experiences of transcendence are waiting for us there. The feeling of godforsakenness is common, maybe universal. The antidote is to place ourselves deliberately in the thick of creation, where we're reminded of our creatureliness and overwhelmed by the sublime nature of nature, provoked to awe by the Numinous. I've sung a hymn to my most special place, a few acres of northern forest sitting on the edge of a lake. Caretaking that land is a joy and a privilege, and it's become clear to me that doing so is part of my vocation, my calling from God. These trees and this creek are my congregation to pastor as a shepherd cares for sheep—they were torn asunder by a tornado, as was I; they have regrown in scarred beauty, as have I. In my 1997 ordination vows, I pledged to be "zealous in maintaining both the truth of the gospel and the peace of the church." These days I'm zealous in maintaining these woods, guarding and protecting them, doing what I can to keep them healthy and safe, safeguarding their peace.

The God of wild places has given us companions. We may be hurtling through space at 1.3 million miles per hour on a little blue marble, but we're not alone. We are interdependent on a whole fabric of creation, woven together with beings sentient and non-sentient, animate and inanimate. We have a unique role in the web of creation, and, it seems, a unique ability to damage it. I've stopped looking up to the sky for help and instead lowered my eyes to the companions around me. My dogs have been my most sacred non-human companions. Seth talks to plants. No matter the species with which we commune, the key is keeping the whole web in view—seeing the forest and the trees, for God's love pulses through the web.

The God of wild places is revealed in the cycle of predation. The whole of creation is predicated on the relationship of predator and prey: plants prey on nutrients in their soil; herbivores prey on living plants; carnivores prey on herbivores. We cannot exempt ourselves from this rhythm. Instead of trying to deny the fact that the cycle of predation is the very basis of existence, I've learned to embrace my role in that cycle and to do so as responsibly as I can.

To pretend that we're not predators is a lie that none of our ancestors would have believed, akin to claiming that we don't breathe air or drink water. They survived and thrived because they were effective predators, and our often conflicted relationship with our food is largely a result of the false denial of our role as predators. If we really want to respect the animals we kill and eat, embracing our role as predators is essential, saying "Yes" to the world as it is and to our place within it.

The God of wild places invites failure. Wild places are rife with failure—broken branches and broken bones, unsuccessful predators and defeated prey. But a fallen tree becomes a home for critters and mushrooms before eventually composting into humus that will sprout another tree. Each failure bears the seed of new life, the rhythm of regeneration that reveals the regenerative love of God.

Failure is endemic to the human condition—indeed, to all that exists in the cosmos, from a star that burns at 35,000 degrees to me at 98.6. The star is degrading, as am I—we're both in a state of entropy, running out of energy, devolving from order to chaos. In other words, we're both dying. And where better to come to terms with that truth than in the woods, among the humus of untold generations of flora and fauna that preceded me? I fall on my knees and let their failure run through my fingers. For their failure—and mine—is giving birth to the next generation of success and failure.

The God of wild place requires risk. We've done everything we can to mitigate risk to ourselves, an admirable trait that has ensured the propagation of our species. But we got where we are in large part because our ancestors encountered risk on a regular basis, and they figured out how to survive it. On a neurological level, adventure facilitates deep learning. On a spiritual level, high-risk situations strip us bare and make us vulnerable. When my ego recedes, there's more room for God. Attaining the next level of success requires taking a chance: climbing a bigger mountain, hiking a more challenging trail, riding a bigger wave, tracking a savvier animal. Modern life tends to inoculate us against these risks, but the God of wild places peels away that safety and brings us back in touch with who we're meant to be.

The God of wild places is in the meat. Ninety percent of us are carnivores, as were our ancestors. The ability to acquire and cook meat played a significant role in our evolution. To hide the acquisition and butchery of our meat, relegating it to places we don't see and people we don't know, is irresponsible, and it denies a core characteristic of our existence. Teaching myself butchery has put me in touch with the God of wild places, with the blood and sinew that is part of my very life. Like being honest about the cycle of predation, butchery reminds me that I'm made of meat, and that in the world as it is, I'm reliant upon meat for my own existence. The sacred connection between me and the food I eat is deeply enhanced by the ritual of butchery. For me, it's a sacrament: a spiritual practice that embodies a theological truth.

The God of wild places inhabits death. Nothing in our existence is more elemental than death. The organism that constitutes me is failing and is susceptible to predators. The same truth is woven through the entire fabric of creation, all of it dying. Keeping this inevitability front-and-center challenges me to live each day fully, wholeheartedly, with everything I've got. And when death comes, I plan to face it without fear.

Being intimately involved in the deaths of so many creatures has attuned me to the reality of death, to its inevitability, and to the astounding drive to survive that I share with those creatures. I am grateful to those animals that have died. They have sustained me physically, and they have taught me spiritually. I hope that my death will be similarly helpful to others.

Some, I suppose, will say I've lost my faith, that I've forsaken the Christianity in which I was reared, that I've become a pantheist. In past days, I would have defended myself, arguing about the difference between pantheism and panentheism, debating the merits of natural theology versus revealed theology. But the truth is, I'm tired of arguing. As Thomas Merton wrote, "If you want to help other people you have got to make up your mind to write things that some men will condemn."[4] So be it.

I did try being a pastor one more time. A friend invited me to work at her church in 2021, then encouraged me to apply to be her co-senior pastor. I pulled my robe from the back of the closet and shipped it off for repair—I even paid to have doctoral chevrons stitched to the sleeves.

Reborn as a pastor, I gave it my all: preached the best sermons of my life; contributed in worship planning meetings; made conversation with parishioners at church suppers. But the congregation didn't want me as their pastor. "It's nothing personal," the chairman of the search committee told me. But, of course, it was personal. They didn't see me as a pastor.

For a year, I thought about that every day, processing their rejection, sloughing off the vocational identity I'd claimed since seventh grade. They were right, and I listened to them: I have stopped seeing myself as a pastor. Brother Merton would probably tell me that I'm finally shedding my false self and discovering my true self.

Where I've found my true self is in wild places, same as Merton:

> If I were looking for God, every event and every moment would sow, in my will, grains of His life that would spring up one day in a tremendous harvest.
>
> For it is God's love that warms in the sun and God's love that sends the cold rain. . . . It is the love of God that sends the winter days when I am cold and sick, and the hot summer when I labor and my clothes are full of sweat: but it is God Who breathes on me with light winds off the river and in the breezes out of the wood.[5]

As I write these words, it's Sunday morning. I'm at the cabin, not in church. I just split wood for an hour (about the length of a church service). My brothers and I cut up some white oak a couple years ago and left it to dry in the forest. I hefted the huge logs onto a trailer behind our side-by-side UTV and drove them back to the cabin. I got the 4.5-pound splitting maul from the garage and started swinging. Crosby sat in the back of the UTV and watched me. The wood split with satisfying cracks, revealing a tight grain that will burn long and hot. Sweat poured down my face as the pile of firewood grew.

I am still looking for God. And I'm finding God in the grain of the wood. I hear God's love in the wail of two loons on the lake, and see God's love in the pair of bald eagles that are harassing them from above.

But I'm not just seeing and hearing God's love as a neutral observer. God is loving me in the grain of the wood, in the energetic force my body requires to swing the axe, energy derived from the venison I ate last night, meat from a deer I killed on this land, a deer that ate aspen shoots in the forest I help tend. God loves me in the ruffed grouse that's walking across the trail, picking gravel to grind up the seeds in his gizzard, eating clover that I planted. God loves me in the balsam buds that, years after I'm dead, will form a thermal cover for all sorts of wildlife in the deepest cold of winter.

I wouldn't say that my understanding of God's love has changed. What's changed is the medium by which that love is delivered to me. What used to come via sermon and hymn and liturgy comes now by tree and plant and animal.

The same goes for salvation. I've only broken down and wept once while writing. It happened as I was completing a series of stories for the newspaper about taking Aidan into the Boundary Waters Canoe Area for the first time. Having described our journey along the Voyageur's Highway—the path taken in and out of the trapping lands by the voyageurs from the 1730s to the 1850s—I looked back on what I'd learned and what Aidan learned. I wrote,

> Someday, I thought, he'll come back here. I hope he'll remember me, remember this trip, remember the fish we caught and the ones we left behind. Remember eating steaks in the rain and me hitting my

head on a tree. Remember the first time he portaged a canoe, that first taste of pemmican, and touching whiskey to his lips during his "baptism" at Height of Land Portage.

Surely he'll remember Crosby, the dog he loves to snuggle. Maybe he'll bring his own dog.

Maybe he'll have a buddy in his canoe and they'll talk about the native people and voyageurs and lumbermen who plied these waters. Maybe they'll talk about burying their fathers.

Maybe he'll bring his own kids. Maybe he'll tell them about his dad, who brought him up here in 2019 and about the adventures they had and the conversations they shared.[6]

As I typed those words, I wept like I've rarely wept. The thought of my kids venturing into the wild places I love after I'm gone caught me somewhere deep in my chest, deep in my soul. I suppose I'd never really thought about it before, about what my legacy might be on my children's lives. So, this will be an aspect of my eternal life: living on in the wild places I've touched, and in the people who've touched them with me—especially my kids.

Tanner, Lily, and Aidan have watched it all unfold. They were each baptized and confirmed in church at the same time that their parents' marriage was unraveling. The oldest video I have on my phone is a grainy, digitized transfer from a VHS tape of Easter morning in the year 2000: Tanner is two weeks old, and I'm cradling him in a pack on my chest as I lead a standing-room-only congregation in singing, "Crown Him with Many Crowns." Now I look at the video of that new dad and successful pastor and think: You have no idea the tornado that's going to tear through your life.

As I write this, the kids are 23, 22, and 18. My more recent videos are of Tanner exploring cliffs in Greece, Lily climbing a mountain with me, Aidan landing a big fish. I don't pester them with questions about their relationship to the church and organized religion, because they need to come to that on their own; they don't need to be weighed down by my baggage.

But I do hope they love the outdoors, that they experience the joy of submitting themselves to the sublimity of nature. That they know they can find me out there in the wild places after I'm gone. And that they can find God.

I'm at a writers' conference in Casper, Wyoming, and, in spite of the fact that my ongoing failure at turkey hunting has achieved near-legendary status among family and friends, I've brought my hunting gear, as has my friend, Mark. We tried to hunt in the mountains of the Medicine Bow National Forest, but a blizzard for which we were unprepared pushed us down from the high elevations. We rerouted to Casper Mountain. To hunt the unoccupied south face, we have to circumnavigate the mountain since the pass over the top is snowed-in.

The backside of Casper Mountain is partly owned by the Cheney family, but a good portion is public and open to hunting. Clumpy red dirt in the lower grasslands gives way to massive PreCambrian rock faces sprouting aspen, pine, spruce, and fir.

I park the truck at the top of a bluff. Bedecked in camo, my shotgun hangs on a sling over my shoulder, and I've got a backpack with snacks, water, shotgun shells, gloves, turkey calls, two decoys, and an 18-inch-high mesh fabric fence that I'll stake to the ground and hide behind when I sit.

I won't need any of this, since I won't see a turkey.

Mark and I agree on a time to meet up and say our farewells and good-lucks—we're already out of cell range. The mountain rises in front of me, but before I can ascend it, I must first cross a deep arroyo—a moat around the mountain, carved by eons of rainfall and snowmelt.

The eastern sky glows. Two goshawks circle high above me, riding the thermals, air already warmed by the sun. Around me, however, it's cold and getting colder as I descend the south lip of the gorge. At the bottom of the drainage, piles of snow defy the calendar, resting in spots that the sun's fingers cannot reach. Cottonwoods, box elders, and willows thrive down here, in the moisture.

I start up the other side. Now I'm on the mountain proper. It's steep, and I have to scramble on all fours, my shotgun balanced on my back. A juniper grows unreasonably in a rock crevice, and I grab it like

a rope to pull myself up. As a parting gift, the juniper saps my hands—
Native Americans use this sap as medicine. Now I'm bipedal again, and
I can stay that way if I lean into the mountain as I hike.

People have long sought God on mountains—Moses, Jesus,
Mohammed, *et alia*. Mountains harbor the energy that created them,
making them among the sublimest elements in all creation.

Casper Mountain is technically an anticline, a fold in the earth's
crust at the northernmost limit of the Laramie Mountain range. As I
walk up this clean rock face, I cannot fathom the energy of the thermal
event 2.3 billion years ago that thrust this mountain 1,000 feet above
the plateau that surrounds it. I feel my creatureliness, subsumed by a
force powerful enough to fold the earth as though it were a piece of
cardboard. I'm an atom on this mountain, chasing another, stealthier
atom—predator and prey. Does the mountain even feel our footsteps?
Does she know we're here?

Psalm 68 in the Hebrew Bible hearkens back to an earlier, primordial time, when gods dwelt on mountains. The language is obscure—it
contains 15 words that are found nowhere else in ancient literature—
and it refers to God with the name *Shaddai*, an archaic, poetic word
that had fallen into disuse by the time the psalm was composed. It
tells of God's victory, and of God establishing a new dwelling place on
Mt. Zion, in Jerusalem. At this news, other mountains grow jealous,
because every mountain wants to house a god:

> When Shaddai scattered the kings,
> > it seemed like a snowstorm in Zalmon.
>
> O majestic mountain, Mount Bashan;
> > O jagged mountain, Mount Bashan;
> > why so hostile, O jagged mountains,
> > toward the mountain God desired as His dwelling?
> The LORD shall abide there forever.[7]

The term *Shaddai* carries ancient connotations of mountains and their
destructive power, but also of the fertility of womb and breast.

God is a mountain, God is a full breast.

Many, many years earlier, when *Shaddai* was still in vogue, Moses was tending his father-in-law's flock. He "drove the flock into the wilderness and came to Horeb, the mountain of God."[8] At the threshold of that holy mountain, God appeared to Moses in the form of a burning bush, gave Moses a mission, and told Moses that upon its completion, he should return to worship at this mountain. Then God revealed another name for Godself, a name that reveals something important about God:

> Moses said to God, "When I come to the Israelites and say to them, 'The God of your fathers has sent me to you,' and they ask me, 'What is His name?' what shall I say to them?" And God said to Moses, "Ehyeh-Asher-Ehyeh." He continued, "Thus shall you say to the Israelites, 'Ehyeh sent me to you.'"

God's name is fundamentally untranslatable, which is why the *Jewish Study Bible* leaves it in the original. The authors note in a sidebar commentary: "*Ehyeh-Asher-Ehyeh*, probably best translated as 'I Will Be What I Will Be,' meaning 'My nature will become evident from My actions.'"[9]

In other words: If you want to know Who I am, look around.

Who I Am is What I Do.

Read my notebook.

The longer I traverse Casper Mountain, the less I care about turkeys. Pale green lichen clings to quartzite. I snap off some sage and hold it to my nose. Scat from various animals peppers the ground. Pine siskins flit between jack pines, calling out with their aggressive trill.

God is on this mountain—in this mountain. I am reading God's notebook.

The last line on the historical marker commemorating Jerusalem Church on Blue Earth County Road 20 outside of Judson Township, Minnesota, where my great-great grandfather William "Machno" Jones preached for decades, reads, "Final services were held on October 6,

1974, marking the end of Jerusalem's 116 years of service to God and the community." Jerusalem Welsh Calvinistic Methodist Church provided a trellis for the faith of immigrants and their offspring for generations. But the time came when that noble purpose was no longer served.

My ministerial robe did the same. That sacred clothing framed my faith, structured it, and gave it meaning. I knew who I was when I wore my vestments. But over time I realized I was hiding in that robe; it provided safety, like a suit of armor, but it hemmed me in, it kept me from growing. To find my true self, I had to disrobe, to take off my armor.

Back in the days when I couldn't afford them, I bought a pair of double tin chaps. Cut from thick canvas and coated with paraffin wax, the fabric is stiff and unforgiving. The first time I pulled them on, they grabbed at the denim of my jeans underneath, bunching the pants up around my knees. I walked with a Frankenstein gait and wondered how I'd ever hunt with these inflexible tubes around my legs.

Today, those chaps are my single most favorite piece of clothing, hunting or otherwise. The canvas behind the knees bears permanent creases. Holes have worn into the cuffs where they rub against one another. Barbed wire has punctured and torn them.

I've worn those chaps through countless fields, where they've deflected cattails and grass and burrs. At the end of hunting season, I mail them to Seattle for the Filson folks to sew them up, those spots now scars that attest to memories of great hunts with great friends.

I've come in from hunts, and the cuffs of those chaps have been frozen stiff with ice and snow, my chapped red fingers too cold to remove them. Other times, they've trailed cakes of mud into the hallways of small-town motels.

Between hunts, I treat them. Laying them on a bench, I scoop wax from a tin and massage the fabric. I feel the wax seep between my fingers as it warms. I aim a heat gun at a patch I've just waxed, and the threads glisten as the paraffin melts into microscopic crevices, the heat releasing a sweet resin bouquet.

I love these chaps. Love is not too strong a word. They are *useful*. They have formed themselves to me, reshaped themselves according to my movements. They are more beautiful with age, their rubs and rips testify to their faithfulness.

A closet in my basement is my new sacristy, where the chaps hang next to a blood-spattered upland vest given to me by my brother on my 40th birthday, when things were at their worst, and a camouflage duck hunting jacket he gifted me on my 50th, when my faith had returned. Boots sit on the floor; they're worn brown leather with rigid black soles, and I don't want ever to replace them, though I fear I must. There's a certain pair of jeans that I like to wear under my chaps and a pullover sweater with a zip-up neck that is just the right thickness of warm-but-not-too-warm. An assortment of hats hangs in the closet, orange and camo, for warm weather and cold, for hunting deer or pheasants or ducks or grouse or geese.

My crozier is a canoe paddle. My chasuble is a hunting vest. These are my vestments now, the clothing I wear for the most sacred thing I do—go outdoors in pursuit of the God of wild places.

ACKNOWLEDGMENTS

IN CHAPTER 4, REGARDING DOGS AND THEIR EVOLUTIONARY connection to humans, thanks to Andrew Root and his book, *The Grace of Dogs*. In chapter 7, thanks to my friend Jeff Green, professor of social psychology at Virginia Commonwealth University, for helping me understand risk aversion and availability bias. In chapter 10, I benefitted greatly from conversations with Rabbi Joseph Edelheit regarding Psalm 68 and Exodus 3.

Some books take longer to write than others—I once wrote a book in a weekend. This book took over a decade. (May Karr is right: events should be seven or eight years past before you write about them.) I am indebted to loved ones who read early iterations of the manuscript, versions that looked very different than the finished product: Kathy Helmers, Lauren Winner, Bob Timmons, Sarah Jones, Silas Morgan, Doug Whitney, and, of course, Courtney. Special thanks to my dear friend, Carla Barnhill, who read and edited and re-read and re-edited.

My thanks to Max Vinogradov for his help on the proposal and to Mickey Maudlin for his wisdom of all matters of publishing and to Aaron Lavinsky for taking such a great photo of Crosby and me.

Jonathan Merritt of the Christopher Ferebee Agency took a chance on me when others wouldn't, and this book is immeasurably better because of his insights. Similar thanks go to Richard Brown at Rowman & Littlefield for his interest and his edits.

Thanks to the first two congregations that invited me to preach-and-hunt: Grace Episcopal Church in Huron, South Dakota (Rev. Jean Mornard) and First United Church of Christ in Gackle, North Dakota (Harry Krause). And thanks to the two congregations that invited me to preach-and-hunt and present the ideas from this book as I was writing it: Lutheran Church of the Resurrection in Marion, Iowa (Rev. Jeff Frohner) and Nordland Lutheran Church in Paynseville, Minnesota (Rev. Mark Kopka).

Finally, my family has been my biggest source of encouragement and love: my mother, Sarah; my brothers, Andrew, Ted, and Cavonte; my children, Tanner, Lily, and Aidan; and my beloved spouse, Courtney, whose photos front each chapter. My deepest wells of love and gratitude are reserved for them, and for my pups: Beaumont, Albert, and Crosby. In the words of Jim Harrison, "He leaves a trail of books, but he really marks the passage of time by the series of hunting dogs he's left behind."

Notes

Introduction

1. Annie Dillard, *Teaching a Stone to Talk: Expeditions and Encounters* (New York: HarperCollins, 2009), 58.

Chapter 1

1. Alexander Pope, *Windsor-forest* (London: Bernard Lintot, 1720), 12.

2. T. E. Hughes, *History of the Welsh in Minnesota: (1895)* (Morgantown, PA: Higginson Book Company, 1997).

3. Cf., Charles Taylor, *A Secular Age* (Cambridge, MA: Harvard University Press, 2007), 98.

4. John Dennis, *Miscellanies in Verse and Prose* (London: James Knapton, 1693), 134. Italics added.

5. Edmund Burke, *The Works of the Right Honourable Edmund Burke: A Vindication of Natural Society. An Essay on the Sublime and Beautiful. Political Miscellanies* (London: George Bell & Sons, 1889), 74.

6. Immanuel Kant, *Kant's Critique of Aesthetic Judgement* (Oxford, UK: Clarendon Press, 1911), 110.

7. Ralph Waldo Emerson, *Nature and Collected Essays*, Lazar Ziff, ed. (New York: Penguin, 2003), 4.

Chapter 2

1. Sigurd Olson, "Fisherman's Sunday," sermon delivered at the First Presbyterian Church of Ely, Minnesota, May 1, 1955. https://www.northland.edu /centers/soei/sigurd-legacy/sigurd-speeches/.

2. Ward, Benedicta, *The Sayings of the Desert Fathers: The Alphabetical Collection* (United Kingdom: Cistercian Publications, 1975), 125.

3. Saint Makarios (Metropolitan of Corinth), *The Philokalia: The Complete Text* (United Kingdom: Faber & Faber, 1979), Volume I, 34.

4. Makarios, Volume I, 169.

Chapter 4

1. James Lamb Free, *Training Your Retriever* (New York: Coward, McCann & Geoghegan, 1980), 41.

2. Feral dogs can be found, but they're rare, and like their semi-domesticated ancestors, they hang around the edges of human society, still reliant upon us.

3. Jim Harrison, *The Search for the Genuine: Nonfiction, 1970–2015* (New York: Grove Atlantic, 2022), 103.

Chapter 5

1. Harrison, *The Search for the Genuine*, 120.

2. E. Jill Carroll, "Predation & the Way of All Things," in Bracy V. Hill II and John B. White, eds., *God, Nimrod, and the World: Exploring Christian Perspectives on Sport Hunting* (Macon, GA: Mercer University Press, 2017), 202.

3. Carroll, "Predation & the Way of All Things," 203.

4. Mary Zeiss Stange, *Woman the Hunter* (Boston: Beacon Press, 1998), 125.

5. Today, however, Fido is fat because those sad eyes still work, and many dog owners reward that look with too many treats. According to a study published in the journal *Animals* in 2021, anthropomorphism is leading to distress and even death among companion animals like dogs and cats. https://www.ncbi.nlm.nih.gov/pmc/articles/PMC8614365/.

6. I, for example, do believe that human beings are ontologically unique in creation, as seen in our advanced first-person awareness, our use of language, etc. For more on this, see the work of philosopher Lynne Rudder Baker, including *Naturalism and the First-Person Perspective* (Oxford, UK: Oxford University Press, 2013). Or, from a psychological-cognitive perspective, see Frans de Waal, *Are We Smart Enough to Know How Smart Animals Are?* (New York: W. W. Norton, 2016).

7. Harrison, *The Search for the Genuine*, 134–35.

8. Aldo Leopold, *A Sand County Almanac: And Sketches Here and There* (New York: Oxford University Press, 2020), 122.

9. Joseph Campbell with Bill Moyers, *The Power of Myth* (New York: MJF Books, 1988), 90.

10. Campbell, *The Power of Myth*, 93.

11. The story of St. Eustachius was recorded by Niketas David Paphlagon in the tenth century and later published in the *Patrologia Graeca* (Jacques Paul Migne, Νικήτα τοῦ Παφλαγόνος, τοῦ καὶ Δαβίδ, Νικήτα Βυζαντίου τὰ εὑρισκόμενα πάντα (France: Imprimerie Catholique, Paris Migne, 1862), Vol. 105, 376–417). It has been retold in many forms, including Eduard von Bülow, *Christian Legends* (London: W. S. Sonnenschein & Company, 1884), 255–77, and in the epic poem *Eustachius seu Placidus, heros christianus* by Pierre Labbé in 1672.

Chapter 6

1. Quoted in Henry Marsh, *Do No Harm: Stories of Life, Death, and Brain Surgery* (New York: St. Martin's Publishing Group, 2015), vi.

2. Revelation 6:7–8, *New Revised Standard Version*.

3. E. M. Cioran, *The Trouble with Being Born* (New York: Skyhorse Publishing, 2013), 17.

4. Pema Chödrön, *Fail, Fail Again, Fail Better: Wise Advice for Leaning into the Unknown* (Louisville, CO: Sounds True, 2015), 45.

5. Cioran in Costica Barbican, "The Philosopher of Failure: Emil Cioran's Heights of Despair," *L.A. Review of Books*, November 28, 2016. https://larevie wofbooks.org/article/philosopher-failure-emil-ciorans-heights-despair/.

6. Postscript: I finally shot a turkey, after I had written this chapter. It didn't happen when I went to Wyoming and climbed mountains for three days looking for them. No, it was far less noteworthy than that—so unremarkable, in fact, that it does not merit the ink that would be required to record it. But if you meet me sometime, ask me about it, and I'll tell you. I still have not shot an elk.

Chapter 7

1. For more on this, cf. René Girard.

2. Agnieszka Tymula, et al., "Adolescents' Risk-taking Behavior Is Driven by Tolerance to Ambiguity," *Proceedings of the National Academy of Sciences*, Vol. 109, No. 42, October 1, 2012. https://www.pnas.org/doi/full/10.1073/pnas.1207144109.

3. Jessica Flannery, et al., "Teens Aren't Just Risk Machines—There's a Method to Their Madness," *The Conversation*, February 6, 2018. https://theconversation .com/teens-arent-just-risk-machines-theres-a-method-to-their-madness-89439.

4. Cf. Kayt Sukel, *The Art of Risk: The New Science of Courage, Caution, & Chance* (Washington, DC: National Geographic, 2016).

5. Rogers, Robert D. "The Roles of Dopamine and Serotonin in Decision Making: Evidence from Pharmacological Experiments in Humans," *Neuropsychopharmacology*, Vol. 36, No. 1 (2011): 114–32. doi:10.1038/npp.2010.165.

6. John G. Neihardt, *Black Elk Speaks: Being the Life Story of a Holy Man of the Oglala Sioux* (Lincoln: University of Nebraska Press, 1961), 272.

7. Norman Russell, trans., *The Lives of the Desert Fathers: The History Monachorum in Aegypto* (Piffard, NY: Cistercian, 1980), 58–59.

Chapter 8

1. Genesis 1:29–31, *New Revised Standard Version*.

2. Josh McDowell, *The One Year Book of Family Devotions: A Daily Devotional for Passing Biblical Values to the Next Generation* (Carol Stream, IL: Tyndale House Publishers, 1999), 253.

3. Samuel A. Berman, *Midrash Tanhuma-Yelammedenu: An English Translation of Genesis and Exodus from the Printed Version of Tanhuma-Yelammedenu with an Introduction, Notes, and Indexes* (Brooklyn, NY: KTAV Publishing, 1996), 29.

4. Stanley Hauerwas, *The Hauerwas Reader* (Raleigh, NC: Duke University Press, 2001), 531.

5. Friedrich Schleiermacher, *On Religion: Speeches to Its Cultured Despisers* (London: K. Paul, Trench, Trübner & Company, Limited, 1893), 36.

6. Schleiermacher, *On Religion*, 104.

7. Rudolf Otto, *The Idea of the Holy* (New York: Oxford University Press, 1923), 10.

8. Otto, *The Idea of the Holy*, 12.

Chapter 9

1. Seneca, *Moral Epistles to Lucilius*, Richard M. Gummere, trans. (New York: Putnam, 1917), 49.10–11.0.

Chapter 10

1. Karl Barth, *The Epistle to the Romans* (Oxford, UK: Oxford University Press, 1968), 36.

2. Clark, Andy, and David Chalmers. 1998. "The Extended Mind." *Analysis* Vol. 58, No. 1: 7. doi:10.1093/analys/58.1.7.

3. My view of human beings—and God, for that matter—as non-dualistic was influenced many years ago by the non-reductive physicalism of Nancey Murphy (cf., Murphy, N. [2013]). "Nonreductive Physicalism." In A. L. C. Runehov and L. Oviedo (eds.), *Encyclopedia of Sciences and Religions* (Dordrecht: Springer, 2013), https://doi.org/10.1007/978-1-4020-8265-8_793) and more recently by the Type-II Christian materialism, a.k.a. constitutionalism, of Lynne Rudder Baker (cf., Rudder, Lynne Baker, "Christian Materialism in a Scientific Age," *International Journal for Philosophy of Religion* Vol. 70, No. 1 (August 2011): 47–59.

4. Thomas Merton, *New Seeds of Contemplation* (New York: New Directions, 1972), 105.

5. Merton, *New Seeds of Contemplation*, 16.

6. Tony Jones, "What Will Echo On?" Minneapolis *Star Tribune* (August 19, 2019), OW3.

7. *The Jewish Study Bible*, Adele Berlin and Marc Zvi Brettler, eds. (Oxford, UK: Oxford University Press, 2014), 1354.

8. *The Jewish Study Bible*, 110.

9. *The Jewish Study Bible*, 110.

About the Author

Tony Jones is an outdoorsman, theologian, and award-winning outdoors writer. He's written a dozen books, including *The Sacred Way: Spiritual Practices for Everyday Life*, hosts the Reverend Hunter Podcast, and teaches at Fuller Theological Seminary and the Loft Literary Center. Tony is a senior fellow at the Making Meaning in a Post-Religious America Project, funded by the John Templeton Foundation, and he is a sought-after speaker and consultant in the areas of spirituality, writing, and the outdoors. He has served as a consultant for television shows, owns an event planning company, and guides canoe trips in the BWCA and writing retreats in Italy. Tony is married, has three children and two dogs, and lives in Edina, Minnesota.